12,

Barbara — this isn't
a good book for you,
Hope you like it —
being an outstanding Texas
lady.
My love,
Alfa

Texas Women

Texas Women
INTERVIEWS & IMAGES

By
PATRICIA LASHER

Photographs by
BEVERLY BENTLEY

Jacket by Vic Blackburn

SHOAL CREEK PUBLISHERS, INC.
P.O. BOX 9737   AUSTIN, TEXAS 78766

First Edition

Lithographed and Bound in the United States of America

Library of Congress Cataloging in Publication Data

Lasher, Patricia, 1947–
   Texas women: interviews and images.

    1. Women–Texas–Biography.   2. Texas–Biography.
I. Bentley, Beverly, 1951–   II. Title.
HQ1438.T4L37   305.4′09764   80–18130
ISBN 0–88319–053–2 (pbk.)

For our children, who will be a part of Texas'
future, Brooke, Andrew and Katherine . . .
And for Bart and Steve.

Contents

Preface xi
Introduction. xiii
Anne Armstrong. xx
Mary Kay Ash 6
Dr. Benjy Brooks 12
Phyllis George Brown 18
Liz Carpenter 24
Rita Clements 30
Lila Cockrell 36
Frances Farenthold 42
Bette Graham 48
Mary Grigsby 52
Shelby Hearon 56
Gladys Heldman 62
Joanne Herring. 68
Oveta Culp Hobby 72
Dorothy Hood. 80
Sarah T. Hughes. 84
Lady Bird Johnson 90
Barbara Jordan 98
Ninfa Laurenzo. 104
Carole Keeton McClellan. 110
Gabrielle McDonald 116
Dr. Alice McPherson 122
Nancy Brown Negley 128
Mary Moody Northen. 132
Dr. May Owen 138

Gladys Porter 144
Lorene Rogers 148
Gloria Scott 154
Jaclyn Smith 160
Sissy Spacek 164
Annette Strauss 170
Sally Walsh 176
Sarah Weddington 182
Mary West 188
Edna Gardner Whyte 192
Irene Wischer 198

Preface

The first interview and photography session for this book began on a sweltering day in 1978 at the Armstrong Ranch in south Texas. Our final meeting was at the Hyatt Regency Hotel in Houston during a thunderstorm and partial flooding in late 1979. In the eighteen intervening months, Beverly Bentley and I carried camera bags, tripods, and tape recorders around the state and, when necessary, to other states to meet with our interviewees in zoo carts and airplane hangars, judges' chambers and operating rooms, executive suites and private homes.

Our initial fear that the women we asked to interview would not be receptive to our invitation was quickly allayed. Some of them, like Liz Carpenter, went beyond the call of duty, offering us bed and board when we remained an extra night in Austin to meet with Lady Bird Johnson. Liz even urged other women to see us, claiming as she persuaded, ''If we don't help young women like them, we won't get into heaven.''

With the exception of former Congresswoman Barbara Jordan, with whom we corresponded but whom we did not interview in person, each of the women in our book worked us into her schedule for at least one meeting, and often several. When additional information was needed, our telephone calls and letters were promptly answered.

Our enthusiasm about the accomplishments and personalities of Texas women intensified during our work. As our research progressed, our only regret was that, because of time and space considerations, we could not include other women in our book. The thirty-six women profiled in *Texas Women: Interviews and Images* represent all women of the state who are helping to create an exciting, vibrant Texas for the 1980's.

Patricia Lasher

Introduction

It is a remarkable land, this once-a-nation called Texas. In a country whose member states, like long-married couples, grow increasingly similar, Texas retains its sense of originality, and Texans retain the belief that the state is, was, and always will be something quite different. It is a belief embraced as firmly by the suburban Dallas bookkeeper as by the rancher who works thousands of acres left him by his granddaddy; a belief sustained by old truths, embroidered with exaggeration, that are deep rooted and die slowly.

For all its monied banks, high-technology corporations, industrial kingpins, illiterate poor, vast and crowded apartment complexes, Texas, in the imagination of many, still calls to mind cowboys, millionaires, cattle, oil, ranches. ''One thing that has always seemed remarkable to me,'' says Texas First Lady Rita Clements, ''is that almost everyone who comes to Texas, no matter how he feels about the state when he moves here, goes out and buys a cowboy hat and a pair of boots eventually.'' Professors and bankers, repairmen and doctors, secretaries and school children have the same goal in mind when they don their western wear during Fat Stock and Rodeo weeks around the state. It is a desire to put aside, even if briefly, the identities that separate people into unions, or classes, or titles and ranks, and share that common, superseding identity: Texan.

The state's early nucleus of people was comprised of Southerners seeking opportunity and immigrants from Europe, who preferred the oppression of hard work, with little government, to easier lives, with political and religious oppression, in their native countries. The ranks of the early settlers swelled with workers seeking jobs, adventurous dreamers seeking fortunes, families seeking homes and land. Today, Texas has its Oktoberfests and Greek festivals, its St. Patrick's Day parades and Cinco de Mayo celebrations, for the people came, and still are coming, from many places with many different backgrounds and cultural heritages.

Yet accepting the spirit of Texas and being a part of its diverse cultural fabric does not depend on a pioneer ancestry, but on an attitude. Recently arrived residents, who believe that opportunities are available, that hard work will be rewarded, that personal independence is valuable and attainable, find that Texas still offers everything that it promised to the original settlers. Although belief in the uniqueness of Texas is fostered today by contemporary promises of economic, social and political opportunity, it was born in the dramatic history of the state and the people who settled there.

School children in Texas are taught early that the men and women who chose to settle their state did so knowing that life would be anything but easy. From its beginnings, Texas attracted the adventuresome, the hardy, the hot-blooded, the optimistic, the able. Those who miscast themselves were quickly discouraged by the environment alone, if nothing else.

For early settlers, the capricious weather was something accepted as the price for a generally temperate climate. ''If you don't like the weather in Texas, just wait a few minutes and it will change'' is not a newly minted phrase. Texans today who see a norther roll over the Amarillo skyline, are soaked by a torrential waterfall of rain in Houston, watch the waves grow tall and angry as winds whip the waters off Corpus Christi, or choke on the rising dust as it dances across the Panhandle plains have a bond with the early pioneers. A test of endurance, determination and optimism, the drouth and flood, heat and wind do not bend to modern technology any more than they did to the settlers' prayers.

When the weather, the hardscrabble land or the sheer loneliness didn't send hesitant pioneers packing for the civilization they left behind, warring Indians and belligerent neighbors in Mexico often did. Histories of the state devote little attention to the philosophical dreams and ambitions of the state's early settlers and leaders. More attention is devoted to their prowess with the gun, their ability to rally for battle, endure siege and rally again. The settlers bequeathed few eloquent political tracts; they left instead tales of action, daring, bravery and gumption. Although brief, ''Remember the Alamo'' was as incitive as all Thomas Paine's pamphlets. Survival was the first ambition, and that depended on equal parts of guns and grit.

The women who came to this wild, new country became partners in the struggle for survival. They sewed buckskin when the last vestiges of cloth shirt gave way. They taught their children to read the Bible by candlelight, and to read Indian tracks by daylight. They packed lightly and fled quickly during the Runaway Scrape of 1836 when advancing Mexican troops sent them scurrying eastward into Indian territory. And they returned to rebuild their ransacked or burnt homes, to replenish their cupboards, and to rekindle their families' spirits. Most of the women assumed the traditional role of womankind, that of raising children, feeding families, providing spiritual and emotional nourishment, freeing their men of household worries. To fulfill their duties, they learned to load and shoot guns, plow fields, tan skins, sleep lightly. Most had left comparative luxury behind for a chance to help tame the new frontier. Many were widowed, forced to survive independently. And, like any group of strong-willed people set shoulder to shoulder with adversity, the pioneer women of Texas produced heroines.

The stories of many of these early heroines are known only to their descendents, who today can recall tales of grandmother's or great-grandmother's acts of bravery and independence. These family yarns, although lost to history, perhaps explain why many Texas men are not surprised when they encounter vigorous, confident Texas women; they may well have descended from similar pioneer stock. Other heroines, involved in the kinds of events that historians record, have become part of the public legend and folklore of early Texas.

Among the pioneer women that history has not overlooked is Susanna Dickinson, who followed her husband to San Antonio during the early days of the Texas Revolution. Her husband died during the Battle of the Alamo, and the next morning Susanna, with her small daughter, was summoned by the Mexican commander Santa Anna, who offered her and her daughter safety and a life of ease in Mexico. Susanna refused the offer outright and chose instead to deliver Santa Anna's message to Sam Houston, commander of the Texian Army, in Gonzales. She traveled on horseback to the Texian's camp where she described, a week after its conclusion, the Alamo battle. Because of her account of the strength of Santa Anna's forces, Houston decided to withdraw and regroup his men so as to lure the Mexican troops into a position more vulnerable to attack by the Texians. Dickinson's story of the courage of the Texians who fell at the Alamo fueled the already intense fires of independence in the young republic.

Endurance, strength, and courage were still required after in-dependence was won, and these qualities are exemplified in the grisly tale of young Mathilda Friend. In February 1867, while her husband was getting supplies in Fredericksburg, nineteen-year-old Mathilda Friend, in her ninth month of pregnancy, remained with other women and children in their small rural homestead about fifteen miles from Llano. A party of Comanches launched an attack, and Mathilda's efforts to defend the small group huddled inside her cabin were futile. Indians broke through the cabin door before she could fire the long, heavy muzzle-loader kept in readiness for just such an attack. One of her arms was pierced by an arrow, but with the other hand she grabbed a cooking pot and brought it down swiftly on the Indian's head. As she was striking him again, another arrow struck her side. A third arrow lodged in her breast.

As she fought one brave who began to scalp her, he stabbed her hand with his knife, and she lost consciousness. When she came to, lying alone on the hard floor with a portion of her scalp cut away, an Indian re-entered and tugged at the arrow in her chest. His efforts failed, the arrow was lodged tight, but Mathilda Friend gave no sign that she was alive. After the raiding party left taking the others as prisoners, Mathilda Friend walked, stumbled and crawled to a neighboring homestead a mile and a half away. A few weeks later she gave birth to her first child, a daughter; she had five more daughters, and many grandchildren, before she died, peacefully, in 1909.

One of the best-known pioneer women, who left a finishing-school background and the comforts of plantation life for the frontier, was Jane Wilkinson Long, known today as "The Mother of Texas." Orphaned by age fourteen, she was living with her older sister in civilized Natchez when she met and soon married Dr. James Long at age sixteen.

When the government of the United States relinquished its claim to Texas in order to secure rights to Florida from Spain (the Adams-Onis Treaty, 1819), opposition to the agreement spread, centering in Natchez. Here Long, an ambitious young man with dreams of empire and wealth, helped raise financial support for the first of several expeditions that he led into Texas to liberate the territory first from Spain, and later from Mexico when it became apparent Mexico was winning its own war of independence from Spain. On his final expedition into Texas, Jane Long, accompanied by her six-year-old daughter and a young servant girl, joined her husband and several other families at the fort at Bolivar Point near Galveston Bay. Promising to return in three weeks, and asking his wife to wait for him there, James Long set out on September 19, 1821, with a small fleet of vessels and men to participate in the liberation of Texas.

As she waited his return, Jane Long learned that her husband had been imprisoned in Mexico. Other men and women left the encampment and urged Jane Long to accompany them, but she refused. When supplies were exhausted, Jane Long shot birds and fished the Gulf waters to feed the three women left waiting. When the cannibal Karakawa Indians began approaching the fort in canoes, Jane Long hoisted her red flannel petticoat from the fort's flagpole to create the illusion that, with a standard flying, the fort was manned. She periodically loaded and fired the lone cannon to reinforce that image.

In December 1821, as Galveston was blanketed by a rare blizzard, Jane Long gave birth to another daughter, believed to be the first Anglo child born in Texas. Finally, after four months of defending Point Bolivar singlehandedly, Jane Long left for Stephen F. Austin's colony on the Brazos at San Felipe and learned there of her husband's death. In the years that followed, Jane Long established two inns in Texas, one in Brazoria which was a meeting place for leaders in the Revolution and another later one at Richmond. By the time of her death in 1880, much of the physical hardship of frontier life had lessened for both the men and the women of Texas. The land that was described in earlier narratives as "fine for men and horses" but "hell on women and oxen" was changing.

Less than twenty years later, a book that detailed the achievements of more than one hundred fifty Texas women was published. Writing in elegant prose, Elizabeth Brooks set out in *Prominent Women of Texas* (1896) to pay homage and tribute to the good women who had contributed and were contributing "culture, energy and good works" to Texas. Lavish attention was paid to women with social graces, charm, style and beauty, and Brooks praised them not only for the physical embellishment their presence gave the state but also for the cultural influences they were quietly but firmly exercising. The work and accomplishment of painters, singers, musicians, writers, journalists and physicians were also chronicled. Although the subjects were daughters of prominent families, wives of distinguished men, or mothers of eminent sons, Elizabeth Brooks carefully established each woman as an individual worthy of having her own life recorded, and she left no doubt that, collectively, Texas women were quite special.

Decades earlier, women at the Houston Lyceum had debated whether women were capable of the same mental improvement as men. Before the century turned, many women had decided that they were indeed so capable and began organizing literary clubs, study groups, Shakespeare and Beethoven societies in which to stimulate their minds and broaden their experiences. About the same time, as community problems in the state's growing towns and cities were emerging, other women's groups were founded to help solve the problems of care for the elderly or indigent, city beautification, and working conditions for women and children.

The Women's Christian Temperance Union, which gathered strength in Texas during the 1880's, was the first state-wide organization to endorse suffrage for women and served as a political training ground for many women. Organized efforts by some groups to attain suffrage for women in 1869 had been quickly rebuffed by the legislature. In the early 1900's, national suffragettes helped organize women's rights groups in Texas, and in 1915 two thousand women congregated in Houston for an all female parade and suffrage rally. In 1917 Governor James Ferguson, an opponent of suffrage, was impeached, and Texas suffragettes rallied behind Lieutenant Governor William P. Hobby, an advocate of suffrage, who replaced Ferguson. In a special session of the legislature, several questions were dealt with, including the question of female suffrage. Needing only a simple majority to pass, the bill became law in time for women in Texas to cast their first votes in the July 1918 primary election, before suffrage was granted nationwide.

It is ironic that the first and only woman governor of Texas was the wife of anti-suffragist James Ferguson, who was barred by the state constitution from holding a public office after his impeachment. Miriam Amanda Ferguson, better known as "Ma" Ferguson, ran a successful campaign for governor in 1924, but her husband set up his desk next to hers and was governor again, in all but title, during her first term. Ma Ferguson lost her bid for reelection in 1926, but was elected to a second term in 1932. Although her husband again ran the governor's mansion, she did earn some prestige because of her efforts to strengthen the state's economy during the Depression.

Ma Ferguson did not run in the 1934 election, and the race that year awarded the governor's mansion to James V. Allred. One of Allred's supporters, who campaigned for him as she toured Dallas fire stations and attended street rallies seeking votes for her own reelection to the statehouse, was a young Dallas attorney, Sarah T. Hughes. Less than a year after election to her third term in the Texas legislature, Hughes was appointed state district court judge by Allred, and she became the first full-time women judge in Texas.

Several years earlier, a strange situation had forced Governor Pat Neff to appoint a temporary "Petticoat Supreme Court" to sit in judgment on a case involving a fraternal organization known as Woodmen of the World. Because the three supreme court justices then in office, as well as most other qualified men, were all members of the organization, they were barred by the state constitution from hearing the case, in which they had a direct interest. When repeated efforts to find qualified men to serve as temporary justices failed, Governor Neff appointed three women to the bench: Hattie Henenberg of Dallas and Ruth Brazzill of Galveston as associate justices, and Hortense Ward of Houston as special chief justice. The three judges, who served from January to May, 1925, affirmed the decision of the lower court, were commended for the brevity of their opinions, and left the bench. For a brief period of their history, Texans had a woman governor and an all-female state supreme court at the same time.

As was true for women in the rest of the country, the American entry into World War II set in motion significant, and lasting, changes in the lives of women in Texas. After Oveta Culp Hobby organized the Women's Army Corps, more than twelve thousand Texas women served in the armed forces during the war. For some women, like Lila Cockrell who later became mayor of San Antonio, wartime service in the Navy brought valuable leadership training. For others, like aviator

Edna Gardner Whyte who trained combat pilots, the war brought opportunities for professional training and advancement.

And women in steadily increasing numbers began to fill the vacancies left in offices and factories as more and more men volunteered or were drafted for the armed services. For some women, this was their first work experience outside the home. For others, already employed, advancement came more easily because the inherent bias toward promoting men over women was thwarted. In 1940, only 22.9 percent of the employed work force in Texas was female. By 1950 that percentage had risen to 27 percent; by 1960, to 33 percent; and by 1970, to nearly 41 percent. The percentage of women in the Texas work force continued to climb throughout the 1970's and reached an estimated 50 percent by the end of the decade.

The influx of women into the paid work force and the political and social activism of the 1960's stimulated Texas lawmakers to review and to change state laws regarding women. Before 1967, the law in Texas viewed a married woman and her husband as one, and the one was simply the man. A married woman could not manage her own property nor could she contract or become a partner in business without her husband's consent. The husband had the right to establish the home residence; if the wife refused to accompany him when he moved, she could be charged with desertion. These conditions were altered with the adoption of the Texas Family Code in 1967. In 1971, the state legislature adopted and the Governor signed an amendment to the state constitution that guaranteed equal rights protection to women. The state's voters approved this amendment the following year, and in 1973 the Texas legislature ratified the federal Equal Rights Amendment.

Clearly, not all women favored these changes in the legal, social and economic position of women. Indeed, some formed active and vocal groups that opposed adoption of the state and federal equal rights amendments. But whether working wholeheartedly for or against this issue, and myriad others, Texas women today often exhibit a confidence, determination and strength of character similar to that shown by the state's early settlers. Many women, like their grandmothers or great-grandmothers of the last century, have made contributions that, while affecting the state's future, will go unchronicled by historians. Others, like those women profiled in the following pages, because of circumstance, force of personality, or the magnitude of their accomplishments, will be recognized and remembered by Texans in the years to come.

Anne Armstrong

There is only a small sign alongside the dark grey ribbon of highway to proclaim "Armstrong," Texas. Beyond a white fence, past cattle crossings and wide swinging gates, there is a small complex of ranch houses where the Armstrong ranch folks live. The houses are warm but not grand. Furnishings are comfortable, a mixture of American and English antiques made Texan with javelina rugs, gun cabinet and worn quilts. Were it not for signed portraits of Queen Elizabeth II and a variety of international dignitaries, or snapshots of Prince Charles in polo regalia, this could be the home of any ranching couple in that broad sweep of south Texas terrain known as the Valley. But it is the home of Anne Armstrong, former ambassador to England, and her husband, Tobin.

Tobin Armstrong is a handsome man, tall and lean like ranchers cast in movies of the 1950's. The fifty thousand acres he ranches have been in his family more than a hundred years. Anne Armstrong is feminine, but not fragile; reserved, but not remote. As she assigns tasks to her secretary, or asks Rosie, the cook, to serve the homemade sherbet, or stops to chat in Spanish with cowboys who have moved several hundred head of Santa Gertrudis into a fresh pasture, Anne Armstrong is confident, gracious, attentive. And when, with courteous firmness, she closes a conversation, she has the barely perceptible, but not unattractive, air of a sovereign, of one accustomed to being in control.

Working in her office at home, dressed in stretched polyester knits with a scarf around her rolled hair, Armstrong is only momentarily flustered when her husband directs unannounced visitors to her desk. Minutes later she emerges from her dressing room at the family house, clad in handsome riding boots and western clothes, her cowboy hat in hand; the handful of people in the room halt conversation and turn her way. Of only medium height, she is an impressive figure with a commanding presence. "We'll have our interview in here," she nods and smiles a warm summons. "Let us know when lunch is ready," she instructs Rosie, and closes the door.

Later her conversation turns to her five children, of horseback birthday parties when they were small, of their varied educational and career interests now that all are grown. She talks eagerly of the approaching hunting season and visits from friends. She is satisfied with her role as an active ranch wife and mother, the only vision she held for herself when she came to Texas as a bride. The rest of her many accomplishments she credits to a supportive family, a matter of timing, and a competitive nature.

Born in New Orleans in 1927, Armstrong was reared by a family that emphasized service to community. Her mother was a Texan; her father, from a respected Creole family. Her great-grandfather had been lieutenant governor of Texas, but this was a family history Armstrong did not hear until past childhood. It was not a political nest from which she sprang. "My parents were Democrats," she says, but qualifies that with, "although I knew that they frequently voted Republican in national elections."

The oldest of three children, Armstrong was a leader in school. "I was competitive in that I was president of the student body in high school, and when I was younger, I always wanted to be captain of the basketball team or winner of the tennis tournament or president of the club," she says.

Academically competitive as well, Armstrong attended both Foxcroft School and later Vassar College, where she was graduated Phi Beta Kappa, on academic scholarship. "I was lucky in having a family that pushed me. Even though we were never poor, certainly my parents couldn't have afforded to send me to the top schools. They made me realize that the best in education was important. Sure, I would have liked to spend the summer playing tennis, but the country was at war and my sister and I were reminded that we owed something. We worked in a burn ward one summer, and I don't think I would have done that if my parents hadn't made me," she says.

During her freshman year at Vassar, upperclassman Frances Farenthold, a fellow Texan, took Armstrong under her wing and "helped to smooth the way. It's something for which I've always been grateful," Armstrong says. During her college summers, Armstrong interned as a reporter with the *New Orleans Times-Picayune.* After graduation, while waiting to assume a job as assistant to the literary editor of *Harper's Bazaar,* a phone call from Tobin Armstrong brought her literary career to an end before it was launched.

"Tobin and I had met . . . when I was around fourteen and he was around eighteen . . . at the King Ranch one summer . . . . I was quite smitten, and he thought I was a brat I imagine, although he has had the good sense never to admit it. I had seen him a few times since the King Ranch. When he came back from the war, he called me out of the blue and asked me to fly to Texas for a weekend. I said are you crazy! I can't afford to fly over to Texas for a weekend. He said he had a cousin who had a plane and would fly me there. Tobin asked me to marry him that weekend, but I said no. I knew I wanted to then, but I figured I shouldn't make it to easy." They were married in April of the next year.

With five children born in a five-year time span ("Don't forget the last two were twins!" she says), Armstrong expected volunteer work, at a leisurely pace, to fill any spare moments. "I did some Red Cross work and I kept the ranch books for awhile. When the Eisenhower campaign came along, I got interested in it rather obliquely. I had worked for a Truman campaign during college, and I hadn't so much decided that I wanted to change parties, but I did think Ike was the better candidate . . . . I went to Raymondsville and in a small way campaigned there. It was a perfect interest because it was so flexible. We had the children, yet I could do a lot on the phone, write letters, show up at headquarters when I could, and be home when I was needed," she says.

Armstrong believes strongly that a mother should be with young children when possible. "It will always be a problem for women. We are torn by different desires . . . . I wanted to lead a normal life as a wife and mother. I could not give that up. On the other hand, I wouldn't have wanted to give up my career. So there is this definite problem that women will probably face in perpetuity . . . of how do you make these things work together without neglecting your children? Another part of this problem is the lack of role models . . . . you're going to have a lot of teachers for a while, male and female, who won't be able to see women as physicists or presidents or heads of universities. Women have that problem too. They don't see themselves in those roles of responsibility particularly combined with families, and they don't prepare themselves in education or work experience to accept these positions."

Armstrong's own career evolved slowly, but steadily. She became vice-chairman of the Kenedy County Republican party and subsequently a national committeewoman and a delegate to the 1964 and

1968 Republican national conventions. In 1972 she became co-chairman of the Republican National Committee. Later that year, she was appointed counselor with cabinet rank to the President.

As the Watergate story moved from the back page of the daily papers to the headlines, Armstrong was called Nixon's "best brave front" to the public. During all of Watergate's suspicions and charges, Anne Armstrong received little criticism because of her association with the White House. "I believed in President Nixon, and maybe if you really believe in something, and you are not devious, it comes across to others. Also, I was so remote from anything to do with Watergate. Never having been in the White House, and not knowing President Nixon that well—I had only spent altogether an hour of my lifetime with the President before I took my job—I didn't know enough to sense the nuances that would indicate something was wrong. Perhaps if I had been there longer, I would have been less naive."

As part of the Nixon administration, Armstrong helped to start the Office of Women's Programs. She is pleased about that but hopes ". . . that some day it will not be necessary and that it will wither away." An early supporter of the Equal Rights Amendment, Armstrong feels that with or without national approval, the goals ERA set out to accomplish should and will come to pass.

Along with women's affairs Armstrong advised Presidents Nixon and Ford on youth and Mexican-American affairs. "Black problems struck me when I was very young, living in New Orleans. But I wasn't aware of Mexican-American problems until I first got to Texas. In the White House I found that the best thing I could do was push for appointments which I felt accomplished a number of things. It created something visible; other Mexican-Americans could see one of their own get to the top. One of the things that changed me from a Democrat to a Republican was that I realized that if you leave people alone within reason, help them to get a fair start at education, language, adequate medical care and things that would otherwise cut them off at the knees and not give them an equal chance, other than that, you are much better in letting the human being soar on his own than having the government or a big corporation or a labor union tell him what is good for him."

In 1976, when President Ford nominated her to serve as the Ambassador to the Court of St. James in London, heading a staff of seven hundred people, she became the first American woman to receive that prestigious ambassadorship. Her name was in the headlines again, as boldface type announced on both sides of the Atlantic that "Auntie Sam" was on her way to England. "The English were intrigued with the Texas part of my background. I'm sure if I had been from some place like Rhode Island there would have been less excitement.'' Occasional Texas-style barbecues helped maintain the image, and even at more formal events she sought to loosen the strict protocol so that guests could converse more freely.

''An ambassador's job, unless you're in a hot spot like the Middle East, is very flexible. If you want to be an entertainer, you can. I didn't, and I think I felt this way particularly because I was a woman. A certain amount of entertaining is part and parcel of your job, but I delegated the details of that to a staff member because I didn't want to be typed as 'hostess with the mostess.' On the other hand, if as ambassador you do a poor job of entertaining, then you do a poor job. Most parties are working parties. When I went to them or gave them, I would mentally have a list of things I wanted done, subjects to bring up to test someone's reaction, people to see. It was business.''

After she left the diplomatic post and returned once more to the privacy of the Armstrong ranch, there was much speculation about whether she would seek a state office in 1978. About her decision not to run, Armstrong says: ''There have been certain things I might have done, they would have been long shots at winning anyway. And some things came along at a time that would have been bad for my children . . . . So I have no regrets . . . . But if at some point my husband says, 'I'm happy for you to do that,' then I could change my mind and seek elective office. At the right time I might decide to run for County Commissioner. I've run for the county school board . . . that's the only elective post I've held. I don't think any office is beneath or below you if you are serving a purpose in filling it.''

Although out of the public spotlight for several years, Armstrong continues to receive daily requests to lecture. She serves on the boards of directors at General Motors, General Foods, First City Bancorporation of Texas and several other major corporations and universities. And she is one of the first female citizen-members to sit on the board of regents of the Smithsonian Institution.

Her original plans for a literary career still lie in the back of her mind. She says, ''If I write a book, it must be an honest one, not sketchy or vague. Right now I am not willing to sacrifice .the friendships that honesty might disturb. Perhaps time will solve that problem.''

Meanwhile, friends within and outside the Republican party speculate over which future ballot may feature her name.

Mary Kay Ash

The corporate headquarters for Mary Kay Cosmetics sits like an enormous golden-windowed honeycomb alongside a busy freeway in Dallas. A wall of photographs on the first floor pays homage to the company's top saleswomen, women of different ages and races whose carefully made-up faces and bouffant hairdos are framed by the mink collars and coats they have won for their outstanding sales efforts. These attractive women, more likely to appear on the cover of *Woman's Day* than *Women's Wear Daily,* represent a swarm of 40,000 happy workers whose combined efforts resulted in nearly $92 million in sales in 1979.

One thing shared by the women in the photographs and those who aspire to appear on the wall shrine is adulation for their queen bee, Chairman of the Board Mary Kay Ash. Barely five feet three inches tall, she is a honey-haired, smooth-talking woman who loves adages: "I'm a member of EA—that's exercise anonymous. If you feel like exercising, call me and I'll talk you out of it." "Aerodynamically, the bumblebee cannot fly. But the bumblebee doesn't know that, so it flies anyway." "When God closes a door, he opens a window." She recites these sayings with enthusiasm and sincerity, all the while smiling at her public relations agent who appears never to have heard them before.

Although a great-grandmother, whose age is guarded as carefully as the secret formulae for her products, Ash has taut skin that is smooth and soft but for a web of tiny lines about the eyes. No, she says, there has been no cosmetic surgery. She is a walking advertisement for her company, and she knows it. There is an element of Hollywood glamour about Ash's appearance; a quality of Texas plain-talk in her speech when, quoting Lyndon Johnson, she says without hesitation, "That dog won't hunt"; and a bit of feminism, hidden behind a Doris Day smile, which is revealed when she talks about the importance of being traditionally feminine but bristles over memories of earlier promotions and salaries she failed to receive because of her sex. She is not one to associate femininity with inferiority.

Her grand top-floor office resembles a throne room. A golden peacock is suspended above the velvet sofa where at least a dozen visitors can sit comfortably. Gilt chairs are covered in Mary Kay Pink. A profusion of porcelain figurines, china baskets, and silk bouquets, selected from the many gifts she receives daily from adoring Beauty Consultants employed by her firm, fill the cabinets. Ash is comfortable in these lavish surroundings and at ease wearing luxurious personal adornments. Her fingers are coated by brilliant diamond rings; her arm is banded with a diamond-studded watch; her lapel is guarded by the ever-present diamond bumblebee who, like the women she encourages, flies because it doesn't know it can't. But Mary Kay Ash never forgets her less opulent years.

Ash was born the youngest by eleven years of four children in Hot Wells, Texas. The family moved to Houston when Ash was a toddler. Her father's health slowly deteriorated, and from the time Ash was seven, she cared for her invalid father while her mother worked long hours managing a restaurant. "I can remember my biggest trouble was shopping. I was given my money, two or three dollars, and I went downtown to buy my school clothes. The salespeople sometimes called my mother at work because they wouldn't believe that a seven year old would be trusted to buy her clothes. After shopping, the big treat was to go to Kress' for a pimento cheese sandwich. Sometimes I'm tempted to order a pimento cheese sandwich when I'm at the Waldorf-Astoria—it still brings back memories of a treat," she says.

Ash's mother constantly encouraged her daughter, often calling her by telephone to say, "You can do it," "You'll make it." The result was an independent child who excelled in the classroom, in the kitchen, in any endeavor she tried. "I guess my mother was doing her best to make up for not being there. She knew other mothers were home baking cookies, doing things for their children. If I wanted breakfast, I had to make it. So she tried to build my confidence when I had to do things that other children didn't," Ash says.

An early marriage that ended in divorce left Ash with three small children to support, and in 1938 she joined the sales staff of Stanley

Gifts, which marketed merchandise by direct sales at parties. Ash wanted income and time with her children; her new job provided both. During her first week she averaged seven dollars in sales per party. But by the next year, fulfilling a vow to herself, she was one of the firm's top salespeople and moved into management. Twelve years later, she left to join another firm that marketed decorative accessories in the home, and she became a national training director in a short time.

Because of a company decision that she could not accept, Ash retired in 1962, became bored within weeks, and decided to write a book for women about direct-selling techniques. ''I wrote down all the problems which the firms I had worked for had faced, how they handled them, and then how I would have handled them. And I wrote down all the good things. Then it dawned on me that I could develop a marketing plan without some of the difficulties I had seen,'' she says.

Her marketing plan was to let women purchase products at wholesale and sell them at retail, thus eliminating middlemen from the operation. Salespeople would be able to purchase their inventory only with cash, either by cashier's check or money order, so that all the income from product sales belonged to the salespeople. ''In too many instances with other companies, Mama would get the $150 worth of products, sell it for $300, and forget that half of it belonged to the company. When the company tried to collect, Papa would say, 'I don't have it; why did you trust her with it?' and Mama would get mad at the company because they told Papa about it. The company ended up with two enemies and no money. With our marketing plan, salespeople have invested their own cash in their inventory, and when they sell it, it's their money to keep.'' Mary Kay Cosmetics still accepts no personal checks from its sales staff. Consultants purchase products, demonstrate their use at a party, and sell on-the-spot.

With a marketing plan in mind, Ash began to search for a product. She considered, then ruled out, arrangements of plastic plants. House gifts were seasonal in sales and did not meet her requirement for a product that could be ''used up,'' creating a continuing market. She also sought a traditionally feminine product, which her saleswomen would enjoy talking about and be comfortable selling.

''I had been using a private label skin treatment for years. The formula for the product had been left to a Dallas woman by her grandfather, a leather tanner, but it wasn't being marketed well. I bought the formula, worked on improving the smell—it was terrible—developed several foundation shades, leased some space, and got ready to go into business.''

Ash had invested her savings of $5,000 in the venture with the idea that she would manage the sales end of the business and her second husband would manage the administrative end. One month before the little pink bottles were ready to move into the marketplace, her husband died of a heart attack. (Several years later, Ash married again.) Fearful of continuing alone, Ash persuaded her two sons, Richard Rogers (now president of the company) and Ben Rogers, to join her. Both left secure jobs to take a chance on their mother's dream. Her daughter also worked with the company until poor health forced her to retire.

The first-year sales were $198,514, and the initial sales staff of ten grew rapidly. There are no sales territories—a consultant from Texarkana on vacation in Tallahassee can hold a party there, sell her products and recruit new consultants. New York and California traditionally lead the list in dollar sales, with Texas following third. Canada and Australia are growing markets.

With enough recruits, a Beauty Consultant can retire from active sales to the position of a director, receiving percentages from her recruits' sales. Some women aim for this move immediately, but many remain in active sales indefinitely. Saleswomen who hold three parties a day, as Ash did in her early days at Stanley Gifts, often earn as much as $100,000 a year, or more. Others sell only enough products to supplement family incomes and to buy extra clothes, Christmas presents or luxuries.

There is a "Half-a-Million-Dollar Club" for women whose sales total that amount during one year. And there is a chance to star, an opportunity to receive the recognition of peers from around the country. This is the glamour, the frosting on the cake, that draws women to sales conventions with the enthusiasm of teenage cheerleaders descending upon summer camp. They gather by thousands to cheer and sing and to hear Mary Kay's admonishment to establish the right priorities, "God, family, Mary Kay Cosmetics" in that order, in their lives. And those who have won fifteen-cent ribbons and plaudits from their peers at local meetings held weeks earlier make pledges and plans to become a top-selling Queen, to be revered, crowned triumphantly, wrapped in mink, and surrounded by a court of runners-up at a future Mary Kay pep rally.

Ash believes that money is best spent rewarding her sales force. While the advertising budget is low compared to that of other cosmetic companies, the personal rewards for her salespeople are great. Watches, typewriters, exotic vacations, diamond pins and multi-carat diamond rings, and the top prize—Mary Kay pink Cadillacs—are part of her incentive plan.

The prizes she offers, along with the opportunity for saleswomen to earn high incomes and to set their own hours, have helped make Mary Kay Ash a living legend to her admiring sales staff. But from the beginning Mary Kay offered more than money, more than glamour, to her sales staff. To her new recruits, as well as to her longtime company generals, Ash has offered a philosophy much like the one her own mother gave her: ''You are capable; you are responsible; you will be successful.''

It's not surprising that her own awards include an Horatio Alger presentation, for she believes that you can start with a little and, with perseverance and hard work, end up with a lot. But Ash doesn't just rhetorically encourage women to set goals and accomplish, to break out of patterns and achieve on their own; she provides both the opportunity and a spirit of community in which to work. ''I don't feel like I'm working *for* Mary Kay; I'm working *like* Mary Kay,'' beams a bee-hive coiffed young woman of no more than twenty-five years, who wants to drive a pink Cadillac and add an extra guest room to her home with her earnings.

And it is not difficult to see how Mary Kay has fostered the growth of her sales staff. Before driving away from her interview in her own sleek pink Cadillac with its heart-shaped side windows and license tag ''Mary K-1,'' she graciously extends an offer for a facial. It is a steamy Dallas afternoon, and the offer draws quick nods of assent.

''Wonderful. I'll arrange for a consultant to call you in a few weeks. You can hostess a Mary Kay party when you get home and invite a few of your friends,'' she says. As she waves good-bye to two potential Beauty Consultants, the sun sparkles from her bejeweled fingers.

Dr. Benjy Brooks

Dressed in a baggy, green operating-room uniform, she looks a little like Paddington Bear as she moves down the hallways on the pediatric floors at Hermann Hospital in Houston, Texas. And the children, if they are able, greet her with the enthusiasm they would usually reserve for someone as dear to them. Dr. Benjy Brooks pauses to caress a tiny, shaved, operation-scarred head in one room; in another she talks slowly and listens patiently to a young boy whose jaw is being reconstructed after a shooting accident. She has operated on more than 19,000 children in her years as a pediatric surgeon. Some of her first patients entered college in 1978, and recently a six year old, who came to her as a moribund infant and has undergone repeated operations, promised her he will go to medical school because he feels she may need help soon.

Benjy Brooks began honing her surgical techniques when she was four years old, performing operations with manicure scissors on her younger sister's dolls. ''I don't remember making a decision to become a doctor. It was the only thing I ever wanted to be,'' Brooks says. She is now Professor and Director of the Division of Pediatric Surgery at the University of Texas Medical School at Houston.

Brooks grew up on a ranch near Flower Mound, Texas, a town she recalls as being made up of a church and a cemetery. She was so anxious to begin school that her mother gave her lessons daily on the back porch, and by the time she was four, she was reading. School work came easily, and Brooks had her bachelor's degree and master's degree from North Texas State University in Denton by the time she was nineteen. "I would apply for jobs, but I wasn't any older than the high-school students. My mother finally said, 'If they ask, don't tell them how old you are,' and she dressed me in her clothes. I finally got a job teaching science and chemistry and biology and directing the high-school band. And the only reason I got the job was because I could direct the band."

When word came in the early 1940's that Brooks had been accepted at the UT Medical School in Galveston, her family had mixed reactions. "My mother cried and said, 'Well, you're going to be tacky. You're going to wear those terrible tacky support shoes.' We had known a woman dentist and that's all she wore. My mother had been a buyer for Neiman-Marcus and was into clothes. I promised her I'd never wear tacky shoes, and then she began to laugh and said, 'It is what you always wanted to do.'

"My mother was probably my greatest model. She just thought you could do anything you wanted to if you want to put out the effort and pay the price. My father said 'It's a man's world and I wish you could have picked something easier.' But then my grandmother, who was ninety-two and had come to Texas in a wagon, came in with her cane. She had been listening to Glenn Miller, patting her foot and swaying her head, but she had heard the discussion. She said, 'Don't you let them talk you out of it. I read something the other day that said the only disadvantage of being a woman is climbing trees.'"

After finishing medical school in 1948 Benjy Brooks served residencies in Philadelphia and Boston and was one of the first women to enter the department of surgery at Harvard. In 1957 she spent a year studying pediatric surgery at the Royal Hospital for Sick Children in Glasgow and was chosen the outstanding woman in Scotland that year. She returned to Boston, but in 1960 when she felt the time was right, she left for Texas.

"I feel that I am first a Texan, then I belong to the United States. Texas is my country. When I left Harvard to come back, one of my professors said 'Stay here, they'll crucify you there.' I said, 'I know exactly where I'll be if I stay up here. Unless you have some untimely deaths or something, I can tell you exactly how far I'll go here. I want to go back to Texas because there you can go as far as you push yourself. I can't stand knowing where I'm going to be in twenty years.'"

The only discrimination because of her sex that Brooks has felt came from students in the bottom quarter of her medical school class, "to whom no one paid attention anyway," and from nurses. Once during a residency, when an operating-room attendant forced her to change in the men's locker room and provided only men's clothing, Brooks' male superior sought revenge on her behalf by going into the women's locker room the following day, changing into a dress, and operating in women's clothing that day. That afternoon a directive was issued stating that Dr. Brooks could have double the supply of operating clothes and change wherever she pleased.

"There's more discrimination now than there used to be," Brooks says. "And it is not from Texans. Texans are used to women being strong and capable; it's our history. It is from the people who come here from the East." Brooks advises her third-year female medical students and her female residents to answer all who address them as "honey" and "sweetie" with the same endearing terms. And for female students, she has bookmarkers on which is printed "The problem with being a woman medical student is you have to be better than the men—fortunately that is not difficult."

"I'm glad to see more women becoming surgeons. I think they have the brains and the hands for it. But it really takes a very, very sturdy body. And women are expected to prove they are strong enough to take it. During my residency, I really made a point of showing I had the energy to go on. If I had a meeting, I'd go and put on fresh whites and splash cold water on my face, and look as ready to go as I could."

Brooks says there are approximately three hundred pediatric surgeons in the United States and only seventeen educational centers where pediatric surgeons can be trained in the United States and Canada. And if Dr. Benjy Brooks has her way, there will soon be a chair endowed in pediatric surgery at the University of Texas Medical School at Houston. Her goal has been embraced by the Benjy Brooks Foundation for Children, Inc., which was established by the grateful parents of one of Brooks' patients. Parents and friends of other patients have joined to give financial support. Dr. Brooks, however, isn't stopping with an endowed chair.

"I would like to build, and that's one of the reasons I came here, a division of pediatric surgery that would take into account the subspecialties of surgery for children the way adults have their subspecialties. I would like to have a pediatric neurosurgeon, a pediatric plastic surgeon, a pediatric orthopedic surgeon, a pediatric surgeon who treats trauma and burns."

When she describes her patients, it is with the words of an artist, not just a clinician. The congenital defects or other ailments are mentioned, but freckles, dimples and bright eyes are also described. She keeps up with her patients' achievements. Former patients have later quarterbacked high-school football teams or been soccer stars. Others are studying ballet, climbing trees, doing all the things that children do. And that makes Brooks break into a broad grin when she talks of successes in the operating room.

15

When operations are not successful, she suffers. "I'm a sore loser. When I was younger, I would keep up a stiff upper lip. I used to go home and kick the door and tear my locker up or go for a ride and cry. Now I don't make any bones about it. I had to tell someone the other day that their little girl was dead. I just cried with them. That's not a weakness to me. How are you going to tell someone that their little three-year-old child is dead?

"You see, after being through a great deal of grief myself, I've changed. All these people come up to you, when you are grieved and the pain is just more than you can stand, and say, 'Well, life has to go on, keep a stiff upper lip,' none of these have grieved. The ones who come up and touch you, kind of pat you and don't say anything, they know that only time, not words are going to help. So the parents and I don't say a lot of words. When they feel like it, after the funeral, they come back and we talk."

For every patient she sees, Brooks says there are often six older people, the parents and two sets of grandparents, whom she must consider. "Two percent of the infants born will need surgery and around fifty percent of all children will have surgery between birth and the age of fifteen. But trauma is our biggest problem. More children die from accidents than any other thing. Accidents, by definition, are preventable, so there is a lot of guilt for parents, siblings or anyone else involved. But there is a lot of guilt when a baby is born with a congenital defect, because everybody's got something in their lives they'd like not to talk about. Like, a grandmother will come up and say, 'You know, I never told anybody this, but I had an abortion when I was fifteen. Do you think that caused the birth defect?'"

Her surgical schedule begins each morning by seven thirty; office consultations begin at two in the afternoon. Her work day often lasts sixteen hours. With interns, residents, nursing students and medical students around her, Brooks is constantly teaching. Her research on congenital defects, burn treatment, spleen reparation and prevention of hepatitis with the use of gamma globulin has brought her awards and recognition. She enjoys teaching, and she has plans for continued research "using private funds because federal funds come with politics. You may be funded this year and not next year."

Dr. Benjy Brooks is one of more than 42,000 people who enter the Texas Medical Center in Houston each day to do their jobs, and her belief that Texans will support the medical community is deep and confident. "This city and this state have recognized that good health care is vital to a community's welfare and to its proper growth, and there are so many individuals who can take personal pride in the medical care that is available in Texas."

16

When she leaves at night and drives to her home nearby, the driveway is often crowded. Her home is alive with her nieces and nephews and their young friends, as well as with her own friends whose divergent interests range from surgery to painting, one of Dr. Brooks avocations. She has not married "yet," she says, "but that's something I might do after I retire. I have a number of friends." House-guests are the rule, not the exception; she thrives on the stimulus that comes when new and old friends, cooking dinner together in one of her several kitchens, talk animatedly. And each year, during the Christmas holiday, she hosts a party in her home for the children of her staff and friends. "Once a year, surrounded by happy, laughing, healthy children—it is a gift to myself and makes me eager for the operating room for yet another year."

Phyllis George Brown

She began the decade of the seventies as first runner-up to a drummer from Longview in the Miss Texas pageant. By the time the decade ended, she watched her husband being sworn in as the Governor of Kentucky and became First Lady of the Blue Grass state. During the intervening ten years, Phyllis George reigned as Miss America, became the first female sportscaster on network television, hosted a network show of her own, married, divorced, remarried, and led a hectic triangular life-style between Los Angeles, New York and hometown Denton, Texas. All this before she was thirty years old.

"People ask, 'Why don't other Miss Americas make it?' Because it's easier to go home and get married to that man and raise a family. But the problem is in ten years, they all wish they'd gone on and done something. When you're hot, you're hot, and you try, which is what I did. I enjoy achieving, I'm an achiever, and when I'm not doing something worthwhile, I don't like myself as much. If I'm working and think I'm giving it my all, I really do like myself. I've always been competitive. I think it's partly motivation, partly drive . . . stamina, energy, discipline. And it's background. I grew up with parents and a younger brother who loved me and gave me confidence."

Like many little girls across the country, Phyllis George would curl up on the sofa before the television set, on that special Saturday night every September, and pick her favorite as the beautiful girls pranced in the Parade of States. And like many little girls, for the next few weeks she would practice walking with a book balanced atop her head, swear off potato chips and take second helpings of carrots to guarantee sparkle in her eyes. But unlike most little girls, Phyllis George went on to win the Miss America title, becoming the only pageant winner to drop her crown as she walked the runway and one of only a few to go on to a successful public career.

Phyllis George has always felt confident, optimistic and pretty. She remembers escaping her parents' arms at age two to prance up and down the aisle at the Methodist Church in Denton. "The minister said, 'Well, well. Doesn't little Phyllis look pretty today.' I knew, even then, the value of a captive audience," she laughs now. Her adolescent years sound like Seventeen Magazine fiction. Her mother, once Posture Queen at Texas Women's College, was a sympathetic ear and motivator, who encouraged her daughter to practice her scales at the piano and do her homework, but also to enjoy life. Phyllis George was a cheerleader, was elected Miss Denton High School ("I thought then that that would be the biggest thing that ever happened to me," she says), and always had a date for the prom.

When a New York friend later asked George if she were a late-bloomer, if it took the Miss America pageant to let her know she was pretty, George said, "You just don't understand Texas women. Whether we're pretty or not, we bloom."

In her junior year at North Texas State University, George competed in the Miss Texas pageant and was first runner-up. "I had so much fun that year. I remember having the greatest time and looking adorable with Buster Brown bangs . . . . The girl who won was a drummer from Longview, and I was disappointed later when she didn't make the top ten at the Miss America pageant. I thought if she won, I'd look better."

The next year, active with sorority work, student teaching and commitments as a fraternity sweetheart, George made no plans to enter the annual state pageant. Although sponsors of the Miss Dallas contest urged her to enter, she said no until the night before the preliminary contest. "A man caught me on the phone and said, 'Would you mind coming back and giving it a try? Just throw the swimsuit in the car and bring your little music stand, and play a few scales and smile and bounce around a little.' "

George won the Miss Dallas contest "a little bit overweight and by the skin of my smiling teeth." But by the time the Miss Texas pageant rolled around, she was ready and the crown was hers. When she left for Atlantic City and the annual Miss America pageant in 1971, she was accompanied by a chaperone, a cheering family, and forty pieces of luggage to hold the extensive wardrobe that Texas sponsors had supplied.

"A lot of pageant winners are completely made over before they get to Atlantic City: new hairdos, lots of makeup, a whole different style. I was determined to keep my own look. But I knew there were going to be forty-nine other beautiful girls there . . . . I needed something to be different, to stand out. So I brought along a pet crab, a live hermit crab, because I'm a Cancer and you know the crab is that symbol. I named him Moonchild, and he had his own little cage with a fancy cover. He was my good luck charm. Everyone took something for luck. Some girls took Bibles; some took a little four-leaf clover. I showed up with a live crab. I also took my peekapoo [part pekinese, part poodle] who sang on command. I can remember going into my interview and having the judges look at each other with their eyebrows lifted, as if to say, 'This girl's really strange.' It was done as a joke really, but it provoked enough questions during the interviews and with reporters to get me through the whole week."

Had George lost, Moonchild might have ended up surrounded by okra and gumbo filé. Instead he went to live with a pageant sponsor's child, and Phyllis George returned to a triumphant homecoming in Denton.

"I think it was the biggest thing that ever happened to Denton. Ann Sheridan had lived there and Don January, the golfer, and of course, Mean Joe Green. But Miss America represents mid-America and that's what Denton really is in many ways. The Chamber of Commerce collected money and bought me a baby grand piano and a bracelet watch with fourteen diamonds in the shape of a crown on top. There were speeches and a parade. It was terrific. They wanted to name a freeway after me . . . . I said no at the time. I was afraid someone would have an accident and I'd be blamed. Now I wish I had let them. It would have been fun to show my children someday."

Packing the Miss America crown and a Stetson from Denton, George left for New York and four years of acting, diction, singing and dancing lessons. "Texas is in now, it's hot. People are looking at us differently now. But they used to think 'Texans, they're just silly. They talk big and walk around with their $100 bills hanging out of their pockets.' I can remember feeling like I didn't fit in when I went to New York, because the people were really guarded and didn't understand openness or friendliness. I remember one night at a dinner party . . . . I was being very 'chic-chic,' and I was saying things like 'Oh yes, I know what you mean, dahling.' The man I was going with at the time looked at me and said 'Phyllis, I didn't meet you like this and I don't want to take you home like this.' "

When Phyllis George picked up the microphone for her first appearance as part of a national sportscasting team for CBS in 1975, her mouth turned as dry as West Texas in the summer. "I said, outloud, to no one in particular, 'What on earth am I doing here?' My own voice brought me back to reality, and I thought, 'You've got a job to do and you're going to do it.'" Although many armchair quarterbacks glared at their televisions when they first saw dimples and a bouffant hairdo where Cosell's toupees usually appeared, George went on to win widespread support and respect during her three years as a sportscaster. She would pour over statistics for hours in preparation for interviews, and her research plus her "gift of gab" helped bring the team of Brent Musberger, Irv Cross and Phyllis George an Emmy Award in 1977.

"I get letters now from young women who want to know how I got started and how they can prepare for a broadcasting job. It makes me feel good to know that they can see themselves in broadcasting and not just as movie stars now," George says. She has established scholarships at North Texas State University and at the University of Kentucky in Lexington for young women interested in radio and television careers.

George left the football sidelines in 1978 to hostess the short-lived *People* program, based on the successful Time-Life publication, for CBS. Although headquartered in Los Angeles, George was again flying around the country to conduct interviews. The program dropped rapidly to the bottom of the Nielsen ratings and was cancelled about the same time that George's brief first marriage to producer Robert Evans was heading to the divorce courts.

"I had to face a lot of things I never thought I'd face: divorce, the cancellation of a show. But, I was living in a fantasy world and reality set in, which was the best thing in the world that has ever happened to me. I never really had that kind of failure in my life, because everything I've set out to do on my own, I've done. I realized that it certainly wasn't the end of my life, and you know, maybe it was meant to be. That's what women should know. If it falls apart around you, you be a survivor. I hope I am, I think I am, and I believe I am, and that's even more important. Nothing's ever going to really get me down. I look for the positive things. I look ahead. There are times when I kind of get down, but working makes me happy."

In March 1979 George married John Y. Brown, Jr., mastermind of the financially successful Kentucky Fried Chicken Company. The honeymoon was not a long one as Brown soon announced his candidacy for the governor's race in Kentucky. Phyllis George was back in the limelight, putting her years of television and promotional experience to work in long hours of political campaigning. Advised by a Kentucky mountaineer that "in this part of the country women take their husband's names," she quickly became Phyllis George Brown, and as that, she serves as First Lady of Kentucky until 1984.

Her political involvement, until that race, had been non-partisan and confined to voting. Immediately following her reign as Miss America she turned down offers from both the Democratic and Republican parties to chair their national youth organizations. Now, with the eagerness that characterized her earlier professional career, she maintains a busy schedule as First Lady. She hopes to promote the appreciation and sale of native Kentucky crafts and to promote the creation of community theater in the state capitol. Legislative bills that interest her include those concerning professional negotiation for teachers and those which deal with sex discrimination and spouse and child abuse. "I want to promote the state, and to do that, I want to be the most visible First Lady the state has ever had. I may already be. That's just my nature and I enjoy that. The most important thing for women now, if they are going to be partners with their husbands, is not to stand behind their husbands anymore, but to stand beside them. My husband certainly encourages me to do that."

Her earlier plans for movie and television roles are not forgotten, but they are no longer her paramount concern. "I'm happily married, and I have a new position as First Lady. I've also worked very hard for a career and I don't plan to give it up entirely. Being First Lady would naturally limit me in roles. I'm still one for the old-fashioned kinds of movies, those that featured women like Kate Hepburn, Ingrid Bergman, Audrey Hepburn. Those were stories with a great message, and the women dressed well and spoke well and acted well. I've never been one for exploiting any part of me, so roles would have to be very, very specific before I would even consider them now. I do have a certain image, through being Miss America and then being the first female sportscaster and now being First Lady. I feel a certain obligation not only to myself and my family but also to the public to maintain an accurate image." With the birth of her first child in the summer of 1980, George added yet another role and image to fulfill.

As for severing her Texas ties, Phyllis George Brown laughs, "Texans don't have to relinquish their ties on me. My roots are deep in Texas, I have family and friends there. I just feel Texas is loaning me to Kentucky for the four years that my husband is governor!"

Liz Carpenter

"You mean I didn't invite you two for lunch!" Liz Carpenter reflects only a moment, then chortles. "I had an interview yesterday around noon. I bet I invited that poor soul for lunch. Didn't give her a bite. Well, come on in. You can sit with us while we eat soup," she says, beckoning broadly through the cluttered kitchen to the dining room. She is wearing a flowing caftan, one of fifty caftans and a hundred champagne glasses that overflow her closets, reminders of her Washington years.

Carpenter has just put down the telephone after the last of a steady series of calls that included brief conversations with magazine editors, quick monologues with participants in an upcoming symposium at the Lyndon Baines Johnson Library, soothing words to someone with ruffled feelings. Liz Carpenter doesn't waste words. They come from her swiftly and accurately, like arrows from a well-practiced archer. And words have been her express ticket to the inner circles of politics, taking her from her birthplace, a plantation home in Salado, Texas, to the nation's capital as a reporter and later press secretary, back to her home in the hills overlooking the state capitol in Austin, and again to Washington.

She was born the middle child in a family of five children. Her father was a former cowboy turned road builder; her mother, "a house-wife, who, like a lot of rural women, quoted Wordsworth and Shelley and Keats to help her forget the dishpan." Liz Carpenter grew up with a deep sense of roots, home and Texas. Her ancestors had brought in colonists before 1823, helped write the Texas Declaration of Independence, and participated in many levels of state government. Many of them had been wordsmiths.

Editor of her high-school paper and author of the Wooldridge School Song, Carpenter longed to attend an eastern women's college. But limited finances dictated that she follow countless relatives to the University of Texas. While studying for her degree in journalism, she worked on *The Daily Texan.* "I love reporting. It was and is a passport to the world," she says.

After graduation in 1942, she moved to Washington, D.C., rented an apartment (nicknamed the "Bedside Manor") with three other UT coeds, and secured a job with a small news bureau reporting on national events of special interest to Texans. "The war helped almost every newswoman in Washington. There had not been many newswomen hired until Eleanor Roosevelt became First Lady. By discriminating, and allowing only newswomen at her news conferences, the AP and the UPI and many of the papers had to put girls on their staffs. Eleanor Roosevelt was hard news. She was going down in coal mines and being the legs and eyes of a crippled husband. Before that, reporting for women had been this business of getting to know the right cabinet wives and uncovering the latest gossip at the tea parties and following congressional wives' fashions.''

During her next sixteen years in Washington, she married Leslie Carpenter, a former classmate at UT, with whom she established a news bureau, had two children, and covered the happenings on Capitol Hill for papers in Texas, Oklahoma and Arkansas. "My husband and I were partners. We were friends before we were sweethearts. When we started having children, both of us were in the bureau, working at equal jobs for equal pay. When a child got sick, one of us could go, and it wasn't always me." (Carpenter still maintains that in order to work, a woman with children needs "good help, a supportive husband and saintly neighbors.")

"And Les and I had round-the-clock conversations about politics. We were in love with politics and in love with Washington. When Lyndon Johnson asked me to go to work for him as a vice-presidential assistant, I had to think a long time, because I knew I would miss working in the same office with my husband. But my husband and children encouraged me to take the job. They felt it was a chance I couldn't pass up."

Liz Carpenter took the job, and in 1963 after Lyndon Johnson became President, she was appointed press secretary to Lady Bird Johnson. Carpenter masterminded press coverage of two White House weddings, organized barbecues along the Pedernales for officials and press, promoted coverage of the First Lady's intense interest in beautification of city and countryside, and orchestrated a whistle-stop campaign through the South during the 1964 presidential contest.

As a member of a speech-writing group, Carpenter added light touches to speeches for many Johnson administration officials. She still occasionally contributes speeches for Democratic speakers, when they seek her aid. Carpenter has written for Mrs. Johnson but says that the speeches are considerably improved by the time they are delivered, because Mrs. Johnson is herself a "wordsmith." "That's one of the humbling aspects of speech writing." Carpenter says.

"I love POWER," she laughs, placing closed fists on the two sofa pillows, emblazoned "Uppity Women Unite" and "Grassroots Democrat," which rest beside her in a bright sunroom stocked with mementos and photographs of her years with the powerful. *Ruffles and Flourishes,* her memoirs of her White House years, stands confidently next to a leatherbound edition of Thoreau's *Walden* on a table nearby.

"Power is what you miss about the White House. 'Get me so-and-so on the phone. This is the WHITE HOUSE calling!' Now that is a big entrance. You know the power is there for just a little while, although you may think you are the only one who ever came there. I think the Kennedys thought they were the only reformers ever there. God! They were so young," she shakes her head slowly with the memory.

"When I review my life, I have few regrets. But one is that I ever went to sleep. I was offered a great piece of life and there were lots of invitations and you just can't do them all. But I wish I had had time to do more. I would probably have spent more time thinking about my family also. Yet they grew up well and they probably wouldn't say I neglected them. Mrs. Johnson made certain that the White House was open to families of people who worked there, and that was an advantage."

When the Johnsons left the White House in 1968, Liz Carpenter became vice-president of a Washington public relations firm, and she remained in the city until 1976. "After Les died, I couldn't stop on a street corner or go into a building that didn't bring back memories of a time when we were together. It had been our town, and once he was gone, it just wasn't the same."

Home again in Texas, she worked part-time at the LBJ Library, organizing presidential memorabilia and coordinating seminars. She contributes articles frequently to several national magazines, and during campaigns she is a popular speaker, lambasting incumbent Republican candidates, extolling the virtues of Democratic hopefuls, always with the timing and material of a skillful humorist. "I believe the Lord endowed me with laughter and I have scattered some of that along the way to all the places I have been—in press circles, the White House, as a speech writer for LBJ occasionally and others frequently, and to the cause which is my tithe: ratification of the Equal Rights Amendment.''

From her Austin base, she traveled often, as co-chair of ERAmerica, to encourage ratification of the Equal Rights Amendment. Relinquishing the chairmanship in the spring of 1979 did nothing to alter her commitment and little to reduce the time she spends seeking ratification. "If we don't get passage, I'll die of apoplexy," she claims. "Women are really going to be angered and dismayed if they are denied such a small request. Everything doesn't hinge on it. But our dignity and our self-respect hinge on ratification. It will make struggles for all kinds of reform easier.''

Carpenter believes that many Texas women were ''turned on to politics'' after the Texas Women's Political Caucus was formed in 1971. ''Out of that we elected six or seven strong legislative types like Sissy Farenthold and Sarah Weddington. It helped both Democratic and Republican women. And don't discount the Republican women—lots of times they're better educated, they're richer, and they've gone to fancier schools. Nationally, they are a real strength, but statewide they still have their problems. The key to the feminist movement is going after political power. We are having a hard time getting women on the boards of corporations, but the only reason we're getting on at all is because there have been some women in politics making noises about it.''

Although a self-described ''yellow-dog Democrat'' who remembers nights around the table as a child when the ''whole family cussed Hoover over a dinner of pork and beans,'' she doesn't let party differences stand in the way of her commitment to ERA ratification. Aided by wit, abundant energy and a firm commitment to her goal, she has an ability to turn semi-interested audiences into enthusiastic ones, well-intentioned supporters into hard-working ones, fence sitters into advocates. She can rally the troops, and her speeches on behalf of ERA are usually followed by an increase in membership, enthusiasm and contributions.

Carpenter is not the first outspoken woman in her family, and not the first feminist. ''I have a copy of a speech my great-aunt Louella made on Salado Hill in 1885. She was a great reader and must have been reading the British feminists. She spoke with gentle words, but there was no mistaking that she was making a great plea for women to be educated along with men. Another great-aunt, Birdie Robertson Johnson from Tyler, was the first national committeewoman from

Texas. She tried to get votes for Woodrow Wilson on his promise that he would grant suffrage.

"Now these women did this with their gloves on, with beautiful hairdos and with a grand style. I think it's too late for that now," Carpenter says. "I don't know what works. Certainly we've tried everything on the last fifteen states. In the middle of the night when I wrestle with what we're going to do, because we're so close and yet so far, a lot of things go through my mind. Conventions which are boycotting the states which haven't ratified are helping. New Orleans is losing many groups at the last minute to Houston. It is hard to get front-page coverage of feminist news, but when you talk about big money, in the millions, which is being lost to a city or state because of failure to ratify the ERA, you make the front page."

It is late afternoon, now, and Carpenter stands, apparently, finished with serious talk. "Did you bring your swimsuits? That's okay, I have a Republican suit you can borrow," she says, leaving to return with a luminescent gold suit left behind by a visitor. "I call it Republican because it is cut too stingy to really be adequate," she says, taking a parting shot at her long-time foes.

Carpenter reflects on her past, talks of future plans. ". . . I have been essentially a happy woman, grateful for the blessings of loving family, good health, a front-row seat on the world, with a penchant for being a part of the action, whether it is as a writer, a publicist or a booster of humanity. I have been shaped by deep roots in Texas, and by the opportunity of being a Washington reporter and having a role at an exciting White House with people to whom I felt a great loyalty and faith."

Carpenter has two books under way, one of presidential humor and another on her personal experiences working toward ERA ratification. But she misses her by-line in the morning paper, and that alone, she says, may drive her back to writing a regular column. In early 1980, Liz Carpenter accepted an appointment as assistant secretary for public affairs for the Department of Education, and again she packed for Washington. "I like my life in Texas too much to leave for long," she laughed. "This time I'm packing in a suitcase, not a trunk."

Rita Clements

Seeking a suitable place to be photographed, Rita Clements glanced around the downstairs parlors in the Governor's Mansion in Austin. Less than three months earlier in November 1978, she and her husband, Governor William Clements, had won the right to live in the Mansion when Texas elected its first Republican governor in more than one hundred years. "None of this is really me, yet," she laughed, as photographic backgrounds were examined then rejected. The shredded fabric on one sofa was so worn that the cotton batting underneath was exposed. In the larger parlor, intricately carved, dark Belter furniture was displayed. The Victorian furnishings, covered in burgundy velvet, sat looking like over-dressed guests at an informal party on the crimson wall-to-wall carpeting.

"The Belter collection is perfectly lovely," Clements said diplomatically, while looking elsewhere for a place to pose. "Actually, the Mansion was built in 1855 . . . . It's what you call a provincial house, so it should have elegant but simple furniture. It shouldn't be a fancy, salon type atmosphere. So what I have in mind is using furniture from the early 19th century."

One of her top priorities as First Lady is to have structural improvements made in the Mansion, using funds appropriated by the Legislature, and to install appropriate art and furniture coaxed from private individuals and foundations. Less than a year after moving into the Mansion, the Clements moved to an apartment for an anticipated eighteen-month renovation period. Since the Clements' marriage in early 1975, Rita Clements has furnished homes in Dallas, Taos, Vail and Virginia, the latter a forty-two acre estate once owned by President and Mrs. John Kennedy, which Clements purchased as a home for his bride while he was serving as Deputy Secretary of Defense.

Rita Clements broke tradition by wearing a brilliant red, rather than white, gown to her husband's Inaugural Ball. But if Texans expected, by that action, a flamboyant First Lady, they were disappointed. Rita Clements said early in her tenure as First Lady that while she didn't want to spend all her time at teas and coffees, neither did she want to qualify for the term activist. She is a reserved woman and enjoys weekends spent at the Clements' home in Dallas, where she can play tennis on their court, drive by herself to favorite shops and relax with friends. By leaving Austin on weekends, Clements believes she has been able to achieve her goal of retaining some privacy for her family. Because the Governor's schedule does not permit him to go on skiing trips as often as Rita Clements—an avid skier—would like, she has continued her trips to the mountains with women friends during the winter.

Clements is an attractive woman: her skirt and blouse conservative in style, length and color; her jewelry modest except for the Texas-size diamond ring she wears. She is described by friends and campaign people as ''intelligent,'' ''disciplined'' and one of the ''shrewdest political minds in the state.'' Some believe that she decided her husband should seek the governor's office, but she claims only to have discussed the possibility with him—the decision to run was made by the future candidate.

Once the decision was made, however, Rita Clements joined the handful of strategists who masterminded her husband's campaign, setting up telephone banks, advertising plans, and the candidate's schedule. By election time, she had visited more than eighty percent of the 254 counties in the state. After the election, the Governor frequently referred to her as his ''secret weapon,'' a title that brought demure disclaimers from his wife. In a state where jokes still linger concerning the strong role that the previous First Lady played in state government, Rita Clements does not want to appear too forceful.

Although she has done the requisite entertaining of legislators and their spouses, it is not as a hostess that Clements intends to leave her mark. Historic preservation, education and volunteer programs are her initial areas of concern and have received most of her attention.

''I'll have to say that when I was at the University of Texas in the fifties, if my friends wanted to take absolutely the easiest major, the snap courses, they majored in education. Now, some of them, granted, probably never went ahead and taught, but others did. So the problems with education that the state has now, are not something that just happened in the last five or six years. I think it's been an ongoing problem, and it's something we have to stop just talking about and grab hold of now,'' she says.

As an ex-officio but active member of the Governor's Ad Hoc Advisory Committee on Education, Clements faithfully attended committee meetings in which various educational issues—discipline in the classroom, federal and state relations, curriculum, teacher certification and training—were discussed. She is an advocate of competency testing for both faculty and students. ''Our Ad Hoc Committee will present a report to the Governor which will be used to recommend legislation in the area of education. It has been time well spent,'' Clements says.

There have been only a few surprises since she first moved into the Mansion. She was caught off guard when Governor Clements on his first official trip outside the country invited Mexican President Jose Lopez Portillo to stay at the Governor's Mansion when he came to visit. ''The only room even ready now is the Sam Houston,'' she exclaimed then. Preparing adequate guest quarters in the Mansion quickly became a top priority.

The volume of mail and requests for speaking engagements was greater than she anticipated, and Clements kept both a social and a scheduling secretary busy answering letters and setting up dates for the more than one hundred and fifty speeches she made in her first year as First Lady. Public speaking is one chore she enjoys. Requests for favorite recipes are a different matter and have caused distress. ''I always had a weight problem as a young girl, but when I first married, I finally lost weight . . . because I had to eat my own cooking. I'm not a good cook, so I ask my mother for recipes to give out. She's a wonderful cook,'' Clements boasts.

As a young girl, Clements wasn't encouraged to learn domestic skills. Born in Kansas, she and her younger brother were reared ''with the same rules, I wasn't treated differently because I was a girl. I got out and worked on the ranch, rode horses, entered barrel-riding and horse-cutting contests in rodeos.'' To avoid the harsh Kansas winters, her father and mother bought a ranch in Brady, Texas, in 1941 when she was ten years old. ''My parents were disappointed in how the schools in the community compared to the Kansas schools, and it was a financial strain, but they sent me to Hockaday [a private girl's school in Dallas] for that reason.'' Valedictorian of her class, she went to Wellesley College, a smaller women's school in Massachusetts chosen to please her parents. In what has become tradition for many Texas women, however, she left the East after a few years and returned to

Texas and the University of Texas at Austin, where she majored in Spanish and minored in history and government, with plans to enter the diplomatic corps. Those plans changed in 1952 when she married Richard Bass, a Dallas businessman and owner of Vail Associates in the Colorado ski resort. Her degree was completed with three hours of political science at Southern Methodist University, but career plans were laid aside for rearing her four children and for civic work. Her political involvement, begun in college, continued.

As an undergraduate at the University of Texas, she had been a precinct chairman during the 1952 Eisenhower campaign, and by the late 1950's Rita Bass was a precinct chairman in Dallas County. From 1962 until 1974 she was a delegate to state GOP conventions, and from 1966 until 1972, she was organization chairwoman for the Texas GOP. An alternate delegate to the national Republican conventions in 1964 and 1972, she was a delegate in 1968. In 1964 she moved to Washington for three months to orchestrate the national door-to-door Goldwater campaign. ''I had worked in that capacity in Dallas campaigns, and once you have the outline for organization, it works much the same on the national level. I helped formulate the program and then traveled to eight regional workshops around the country to help explain the door-to-door campaigning. Then I spent the next two months on the phone with state chairmen.'' During the Nixon administration, she served on the Advisory Board for Action which supervised VISTA and the Peace Corps. She was a Republican national committeewoman from 1973, the same year she and Bass were divorced, until 1975 when she married William Clements and resigned her post because her new husband was serving as Deputy Secretary of Defense.

''Until I became a national committeewoman, I really only worked hard at election time. I was not a year-round political worker. During elections, I worked real hard for three or four months and then I'd say goodbye. Then two years later, I'd get involved again.''

She was also active in community work through her involvement with the Junior League of Dallas and was president of the Dallas organization for several years. When she became First Lady, Clements was on the Board of the United Way of Dallas, the Winston School and the Fine Arts Committee of the Department of State.

''I have a strong personal feeling that we get a lot from this country and we should try to give a lot back to it. I have always felt that it is important for citizens to particiapte, and through participation in politics, we can shape the government we have. I definitely believe in a free enterprise system. Private initiative should stay in private hands, and the role of government, I believe, at the federal, state and local level is to protect and defend its citizens and not to take over functions best left to private individuals and concerns. I've always wanted to be involved, to contribute, and politics has been one way that I could,'' she says.

But Clements says she has never seriously considered running for public office herself. ''The circumstances have never really been such that I felt I could run for office. I've had too many other responsibilities. And I guess I'm too sensitive. I let criticism bother me. Bill just lets criticism fall off his back; he figures he's got to take it, it goes with the job. When he gets criticism, it bothers me, though not as much as it used to, because I see that he can take it.''

While she doesn't intend to run for office herself, Clements says that the opportunities for women to seek elective office in the state have improved dramatically in the past decade. ''I think women no longer have to apologize for getting out and working and doing things in what has traditionally been a man's world. If I were the age of my twin girls [Bonnie and Barbara Bass were 1979 graduates of Stanford] just starting out . . . well, it's an exciting time for women.''

Lila Cockrell

Delayed by a ribbon-cutting ceremony, Lila Cockrell marched past the front door of her city hall office. She nodded with a smile that acknowledged, yet discouraged conversation with, the citizens who were assembled in the waiting room. Within minutes she was stationed behind her desk, and by mid-afternoon, appointments were back on schedule. She is an efficient, diligent woman, the type people trust to manage their tax dollars. It was her reputation as a hard worker, and not a flair for flamboyant political campaigning, that helped her win the mayor's job in San Antonio in 1975.

Many of the objectives that Lila Cockrell outlined in her first race have been achieved. Tourism, with its tourist dollars and increased local employment, is growing steadily; public transportation is improving; the downtown business district is being revitalized. The goal she sets now for herself and Texas' third largest city is to expand San Antonio's economic base, not only by bringing in new industry but also by improving the climate for expansion of existing business. Hardcore unemployment, substantial poverty, and provision of basic education and adequate housing are the major problems she sees facing her city in the 1980's.

As a three-term mayor of a major city, Cockrell talks without hesitation about federal revenue sharing and development grants, budgeting and finances. But when first elected a city official in 1963, she wasn't so confident. "While I had been active in the League of Women Voters, I had never been a business leader. I felt less confident initially in the areas of budget and finance and more comfortable in the

37

areas of parks, libraries, issues that would be considered traditionally women's issues. Then I started studying. I felt that if I was going to be a good council member, I didn't want to operate in just a few areas of government. I wanted to learn all of it, all that I needed to know.''

Cockrell's interest in politics and government goes back even further than her long-time commitment to the League of Women Voters. Her parents lived in San Antonio, but her mother, quite young at the time, went to her parents' home in Ft. Worth just before Cockrell's birth. A year and a half later, Lila Cockrell's father died. Although she lived for periods of time with her mother, who remarried and lived in New York, most of her childhood and adolescent years were spent with her grandparents in Ft. Worth, where her budding political consciousness was nurtured by her outspoken grandmother.

"My grandparents were very devout Republicans, and as a child you are indoctrinated into the family position. In one of the presidential elections when I was about five years old, I remember gathering up all the neighborhood children and leading the parade. I had handpainted signs and all these children in the parade were carrying signs for the Republican presidential candidate. The only problem was that all the other families were Democrats. One by one, the parents of the neighborhood came and snatched their child out of the parade. Finally the parade disintegrated and there was just me,'' she laughs. Later, in high school, when an all-male oratory group called the Senate refused to allow women to join, Cockrell organized an all-female counterpart, which she called the Little Congress.

Her love for oratory developed in childhood as she listened spellbound to her grandmother deliver impassioned and articulate speeches for temperance. "I would say that my grandmother was the person in my life who really made the difference. She was a very, very active woman, especially for the cause which was important to her and that was temperance. She was always president of the Women's Christian Temperance Union. She was a very loyal follower of Frances Willard, who had been the leader in the temperance movement. But aside from the specific issue which was important to her, I think I was influenced by the whole idea of her attitude of being interested in a cause and feeling as a woman that you had a right, an obligation, to speak out and to become involved. She would go around and make speeches when many women were not doing that . . . . So, to me, the League of Women Voters became what the WCTU had been to her. It was the organization that I enjoyed and found able to give creative leadership.''

Shortly after graduation from Southern Methodist University, with a degree in speech, the future mayor married S. E. Cockrell. When her husband went overseas during World War II, Lila Cockrell applied and was accepted as an officer candidate for the WAVES. As the commanding officer of a company of WAVES judged "best commanded and performed" in the Bureau of Ships, Ensign Cockrell received an Award of Recognition before she left the service.

Following the war, the Cockrells settled in Dallas, and in the spare time left after caring for her family, Lila Cockrell worked with the League of Women Voters and eventually served as president of the Dallas organization. But when her husband was named executive director of the Bexar County Medical Society in the late fifties, she moved her family to San Antonio with the idea of "minding my own business, remaining at home and perhaps learning to sew . . . . I found out that I didn't like that one bit!" She had met several leaders of the San Antonio League of Women Voters at state and national conventions, and they soon began looking her up. "I became active again. Once I start participating, I have a tendency to start speaking out, becoming involved, offering suggestions and ideas. First thing you know, you're in some kind of leadership role."

Cockrell has been described by some who have worked with her as the "ultimate club woman." Years of work with such organizations as parent and teachers groups, religious associations, and the League of Women Voters have given her a reputation of being reliable, diplomatic, thorough, even-tempered and reserved to the point of occasionally appearing aloof. She is not known for hasty decisions, or for taking unpopular stands. When she was tapped to run for San Antonio city council as part of the Good Government League's slate of candidates, other club women rallied to her support by organizing door-to-door canvassing, telephone banks, leafleting. "I wasn't exactly a token," she says now, "but I think the general consensus was that it was time to put a woman on the council. At that time the GGL sponsored what was nearly always a winning team for the City Council."

She first discussed the candidacy with her husband and two teenage daughters. "They were very conservative about it. My husband tends to be protective and my daughters were then very worried because nobody else's mother had ever done that." But the family eventually supported her decision to run.

Cockrell served on the council until 1970, retired to private life for three years, then was re-elected in 1973. As her last term was ending, she decided to run for mayor. "If you're on the council, and you have ideas and want to get certain things done, then you want to be mayor. Over and over, I heard people say things like 'Lila, you would sure make a great mayor if only you were a man.' And they were saying it not in a derogatory sense, but really as sort of a compliment.

Yet they felt this limitation. So when I first became mayor in 1975, [after defeating beer distributor John Monfrey in a fiercely fought campaign] I realized objectively that there were persons who wondered if I would have the toughness that is sometimes required in the mayor's position.

"You can be pleasant, you can be conciliatory, you can work with people, but there are times when you just have to be tough. I try to be tough and ladylike at the same time. I try to be firm when I need to be firm, and I also try to make decisions that are sensible, that are the right decisions based on the facts at hand and not just emotional decisions."

While the mayor's job still has its ceremonial functions, the days are gone when the mayor simply turns over the first spadeful of dirt or cuts the ribbon on a completed project. "The change," Cockrell says, "occurred during the 1960's when we got into these direct relationships with the federal government. I guess it really started changing with the war on poverty program. Back in the 1950's when we first started council-member government in San Antonio, government was just housekeeping. You collected your garbage; you had your police, your fire department, your public works department, and you maintained your airport. You kept house. But in the sixties, it became a matter of policy leadership. And that's when the role of the mayor changed. When you have community development block grants, revenue sharing, public works monies coming down from Washington, then you get involved in leadership roles, and not just in your own city. With the U. S. Conference of Mayors, the Texas Municipal League and other organizations, the role of mayor becomes increasingly important because the decisions of these organizations can greatly affect what happens in your own city."

Cockrell has expressed cautious concern locally and nationally about the effects of growth on the Sun Belt. "I think that in an area that is growing, and particularly areas that are growing rapidly, you have to be careful not to fall into some of the same problems that have occurred in the older, industrialized areas in the North and Northeast. You can find yourself . . . in the future with a city that has an aging inner-structure, and where industries begin leaving your city to move on to greener pastures somewhere else. We have to look, as we are growing, not just at the short-term but also at the long-term ability of the city and the state to integrate these new economic resources that are coming in, and make them a long-term, stable part of our community."

Until Chicagoans elected Jane Byrne their mayor, San Antonio was the largest city in the country with a woman leading the city government. And the fact that she is a woman is no longer an issue, Cockrell believes, during election time. Even the school children whom she makes an effort to meet ("I love to be with the young people and take time with them so they will have respect for public officials.") are accustomed to their city having a female mayor. "Occasionally my husband and I will be together with people from other cities and someone will say 'There's the mayor,' and they will run over and shake his hand," she laughs.

Lila Cockrell believes that Texas is not far from the day when a woman governor will be elected, citing difficulty in raising funds as the only major obstacle for politically ambitious women. She points out that numerous young women are moving into the mainstream of local and state government, as appointed and elected officials. But she does not foresee the development of a separate political power base—an "old girl" network—for women in Texas.

"There have been several tentative efforts in that direction, and none of them have been very successful. I think the reason is that we didn't like the 'old boy' system, and you know, do you want to replace it with an 'old girl' system? I would rather have an integrated system where, for example, in my supporters I can count on both men and women. And I can count on heavy contributions now, for the first time, from substantial segments of the business community because they have confidence in me.

"The women of Texas don't need an 'old girl' system. I think Texas women are strong; they have a lot of pioneer spirit. I think that, through the years, Texas women, many of them—no generalizations, not all but many of them—have through force of circumstances had to take strong positions, strong roles. I think they are not afraid and they do not hold back."

Frances Farenthold

When weather permitted and its owner was in residence, the state flag of Texas flew over the office of Wells College president Frances "Sissy" Farenthold in Aurora, New York. There was a time in 1972 when a scrappy band of reform-conscious Democrats hoped to see Farenthold under the state flag at the governor's office in Austin. The primary election was close enough to throw her into a runoff with Dolph Briscoe, but the zealous efforts of her supporters—college students and liberal attorneys, blacks and chicanos, women, young and old—could not defeat the well-funded, more conservative Briscoe. Later that year at the National Convention in Miami Beach, as the first woman ever nominated and voted upon for vice-president, Farenthold received four hundred delegate votes, before bowing out to Thomas Eagleton.

During the next four years Farenthold served as an assistant professor of law at Texas Southern University and at the University of Houston, became the first chairperson of the National Women's Political Caucus, which she had helped organize, and made a second, less spirited and unsuccessful attempt at the governor's office. In 1976 she became the first woman president of Wells College, a small college for women in New York.

When Farenthold first glanced around her presidential office at Wells, portraits of her twelve male predecessors leveled eyes at her like a jury. Undaunted, she had the portraits moved to the college library. "There wasn't a role model among them," she recalls. During her four-year presidency, Farenthold was instrumental in securing a $250,000 grant, shared by five universities and colleges, to create a network of programs aimed at helping women enter politics and run for political office, thus encouraging the role models that she believes are so important to young women.

Farenthold assumed her job at Wells College with a promise to her supporters that she would not become inactive politically. The Republican strength in tiny Aurora provided little support for her Democratic leanings. Working at the polls in one election, she was one of less than a half dozen voters to participate in a Democratic primary. She faded from the visible political scene, but she says, ''So long as you use the First Amendment, you are active politically,'' and speaking engagements around the country kept her in touch with a variety of political groups.

As Farenthold informally talks about her early political efforts, it is difficult to imagine her before a podium. Her voice is shy, so soft-spoken that listeners must lean forward to catch words. It rises in intensity when she talks of injustices yet to be erased, of social problems being ignored by government and citizens. Talking about lost races and hard-earned victories, she has the quiet, resigned air of one who has fought successful battles, yet still waits to win the war.

During a quick trip away from Wells to Houston, where she will address a convention, grant several interviews and visit hurriedly with her husband and a few close friends, Farenthold looks tired. ''I've thought about slowing down. I've had to sacrifice things like the simple courtesy you show friends by visiting when they are sick. But my chronic condition is restlessness, searching. Sometimes I'd like to stop, but that doesn't last long. Whenever I think about living a slower pace, I also think about how quiet things will be in the grave,'' she murmurs with a wry smile.

''With all of it, and I've had some difficult times, I'd still take it . . . . Until I went to Austin [to the legislature] I was living five blocks from where I was born. I never expected to leave there. These times for most women have really been uncharted; my life certainly has been. I'm afraid I contradict my advice to women students about planning their lives,'' she says.

Farenthold was reared to believe in social reform and active participation in government. Her father, a Corpus Christi lawyer, encouraged his daughter to accompany him to the courtroom after her classes. After her three-year-old brother died when she was two, many of the traditional expectations a parent has for a first-born son were shifted to young Sissy. In addition, because her mother was sick and often hospitalized for long periods of time, Sissy assumed much of the

44

responsibility of running the household staff. Family friends have told her that at age eight she was directing caterers to the silver closet and pantry when her parents entertained.

As early as junior high school she felt the bitter sting of the lost election. When she recognized the discrimination against Mexican-American students in the classrooms, she attempted to organize them into a coalition that would support her in her race for class treasurer. "I lost by the largest majority that anyone had ever lost by, and lost to a football star," she groans. "It kept me from running for anything again until I was a grown woman with children."

She was a brilliant student and graduated from Hockaday Preparatory School in 1943, from Vassar College in 1946, and from the University of Texas Law School in 1949 before joining her father's firm. Farenthold set aside her law career once she married and began raising children, not knowing that her father continued to pay her Bar Association dues should she change her mind and return to the courtroom. She was active in her church and served as president of the deanery of the National Council of Catholic Women. When one of her five children, the twin brother of her son Jimmy, died at age four in 1960, she sought activity to assuage the sorrow. Originally she set a limit of ten years to "do something in politics." She became a member of the Corpus Christi Human Relations Commission and director of Legal Aid for Nueces County.

Then she turned her sights toward party politics. All she wanted initially was to be county secretary of the Democratic party. "I asked a friend about that job, and he said 'I could support you for secretary. But someday you might decide to run for chairman of the party and we just couldn't have a woman serve as county chairman.' If there had been a place for me in the county party structure, I'd probably never have run for office," she says.

Not long afterward, in 1968, at the urging of both her husband and her father, she ran for the Texas House of Representatives and was elected. "If I had been willing to remain a pet, there would probably have always been a place for me there," she says. "I was given a bow tie by the Speaker and on Valentine's Day the poet laureate of the House read a poem to me. I could have been the 'little lady from Corpus.' If I had accommodated that and stayed with issues like education and tax advantages for ladies' charitable groups, it would have been fine with them." Instead, Farenthold became the unofficial den mother of a pack of reform warriors soon dubbed "The Dirty Thirty."

"I really set out first just to get an investigative study in the legislature. I had an academic interest as a student of government in seeing how we, the rank and file, could sit there in the legislature and pass special interest legislation, the banking bills for example, without understanding or knowing it,'' she says. ''We didn't get the study, but when it was all over, the leadership toppled and we had the 'Sharpstown Investigation.' There was a lot of talk, but all we really did accomplish were some limited procedural reforms, some exposure of interest group activities and some reform in reporting of testimony before committees.''

During her presidency at Wells, Farenthold was credited with several major achievements including a balanced budget with a modest surplus, a new athletic facility, enrollment increases, an energy conservation program and the opening of a full-time women's career counseling office. She encouraged students to participate in athletics, arguing that participation in sports makes women more competitive and tougher. Another project she started allows students to complete three years of study in mathematics or science at Wells, then two years at Texas A&M in petroleum engineering, before receiving a bachelor's and a master's degree.

Her strong advocacy of women's colleges has been reinforced by her experience. ''There continues to be so much discrimination in general, and much is reflected in institutions of higher learning. There are overt biases in the marketplace, but there are biases too in the academic world. At a women's college or university, young women have an opportunity to assess themselves outside the traditional society. I've told them during their first year, you have to claim, not receive, education, and you have to put some planning in your lives. I know personally that I wouldn't have survived the University of Texas Law School without the confidence I gained at Vassar,'' she claims. ''You have to speak up in a classroom in a women's college.''

In October 1979, on her twenty-sixth wedding anniversary, Farenthold announced that she would retire from the presidency of Wells at the end of the academic year and return to Texas to practice law in Houston. She did not rule out the possibility of once again seeking public office. Months earlier, however, she had mused philosophically: ''I might run again. Nixon should have taught us never to say 'Never.' But I'm not in step with the times now. The problems of the next person are not our concern now, and you are safe, politically, if you continue to trample on those who have less than others. I see I'm not part of that, for better or worse, and I couldn't be in step with that. So in a sense, there really isn't any place for me,'' she sighs, her regret focused more on her concern for others than any personal ambition.

Time and experience have affected Farenthold, who recognizes a loss of idealism in herself and a greater awareness of the limits to

46

change. "I had a big slice of naivete in me years ago. I've learned that things move more slowly, and it is not as simple to bring about change as I had hoped. There are so many competing aspects, entrenched bureaucracy, defined opinions. At the same time, I'd repeat what I said years ago, that if the people knew how much power they had, they'd have more. They have the process; it's still there. It is getting so much more difficult to compete unless you really have a ground swell of support. With the Lear jet, computers, speech writers, all the resources against you if you don't have the money, it is more difficult. Now you go out and see what's palatable to the people and that's what you say to them. I have no tolerance for that. I can't buy that. You can call me a knee-jerk liberal, a bleeding heart. I'm just out of step with the majority feelings today."

48

Bette Graham

Bette Graham is long in answering the doorbell, explaining when she finally appears that she was in the midst of an important telephone conversation. Her voice is soothing to hear, a pleasant blend of long, low Texas tones influenced by her San Antonio childhood and her many years in Dallas. She accepts compliments on her large home with shy, modest pride. There is little about her appearance or her environment to suggest that she once invented a product that revolutionized secretarial work. It is difficult to imagine her in the boardroom of a multimillion-dollar corporation; far easier to envision her laboring over the sculptured figures which are displayed in her home. But there was a less affluent point in her life, nearly twenty-five years ago, when her basic desire to "do a good job" led her to experiment her way into the business world.

When electric typewriters were introduced into her office in 1954, Bette Graham, an efficiency-conscious executive secretary, worried. Finding the new machines so sensitive to her touch that she spent an increasing portion of her time correcting errors, Graham pondered a method of covering rather than erasing an error. An artist by hobby, she began mixing tempera paints with other chemicals in her kitchen. After a kitchen fire, many ruined saucepans, and frequent nights without sleep as she worked late, Graham came up with an effective concoction. She put some into a jar and brought it with a watercolor brush to her office. Soon secretary friends were asking for a supply.

"I began to realize that there was a great need for it. I ordered bottles and made my own labels . . . it was Mistake Out then. I continued trying to develop a better product. I didn't know much about chemistry but I knew I wanted a pigment in solution that was opaque and would dry faster than the original product did. I went to the libraries and researched, and I wrote to chemical companies for samples of products . . . they were very helpful. A chemist I knew worked with me on Saturdays.''

All the while Graham continued with her job as a secretary. Supplies and paid assistance for her experimentation came from her $350-a-month salary, which also had to support herself and her son because her first marriage had ended in divorce shortly after World War II. She had seen her mother overcome similar circumstances following a divorce and start a small business. Of her own efforts, Graham says, ''It was hard to manage, but I felt, and I still feel, that the best way for a company to grow is through its own productivity, its own efforts, and not on a lot of borrowed money. I feel that growing through your own inventiveness . . . . brings an element of order and substance to the company that doesn't develop otherwise.''

By 1958, Graham had resigned her secretarial position to devote full time to wide-scale marketing of her premier product, Liquid Paper, those tiny black-and-white bottles that found their way into every secretary's top drawer. Production moved from a backyard enterprise, where her son Michael Nesmith, later a member of the rock group The Monkees, filled bottles, to an elaborate office facility and production plant with national distribution. The company incorporated in 1965 and became Liquid Paper Corporation in 1968.

''Bloom where you are planted,'' she has often advised, and in an effort to create a working environment in which each employee can reach what Graham calls ''Full Usefulness,'' she helped design a building with park areas, fine arts and a library when Liquid Paper moved into new offices in 1972. Her goal was to create ''a place where the plant worker and office worker can get to know each other, where ideas can be exchanged.'' Committees, she says, played an important role in the development of her company. Employees from different levels of the company rotated on these committees and participated in decisions on operations and marketing.

And just as she had aimed her product at women, Graham took steps to encourage more women to find their places in the business community. In 1976, with royalties from the formula for her Liquid Paper, Graham established the Bette Clair McMurray Foundation. Established in her maiden name, the foundation awards approximately $200,000 in grants annually for projects that promote recognition, equality, and solidarity among women and that encourage a balance between opportunities for men and women, without displacing one or the other.

When she talks about opportunities for women in business, it is with a spiritual, rather than a militant, note to her calm voice. Raised a Methodist, Graham became a Christian Scientist in 1942, and her deep religious convictions have shaped her business philosophy. While she is a "feminist who wants freedom for myself and everybody else," her interest in bringing women into business is more than a desire for equal rights. She has long held the belief that business left only in the hands of men often takes on a "brutish" quality, an attitude of "as long as it is not illegal, it is all right to do something." Women, Graham believes, bring "nurturing, love and grace" to the business world, and once women have taken their place alongside men, these qualities will become ingrained in business.

In 1962 she married Robert Graham, and together they worked on expanding the product line and increasing their market. Bette Graham resigned as president of the corporation in 1968 to become chairman of the board. In 1975, after a divorce from Robert Graham, she resigned from the board and he assumed the top position. She became a full-time Christian Science Practitioner, an activity she describes as "the highest kind of work." She is listed in the *Christian Science Journal* and receives calls day and night from fellow Christian Scientists who are in need.

Of her decision to resign from the Liquid Paper board, Graham says in retrospect, "It was a stupid thing to do, a stupid thing. My husband had left me," and she explains, "It was very difficult for me to work with him . . . . But I would never have resigned if I had known that the philosophy of personal and corporate growth on which I founded the company would not be carried out."

Another area of contention, she says, was the board's decision to change the formula for Liquid Paper, which deprived her of royalties. The royalty matter was resolved in 1979 with the company's sale. Her ownership of nearly half of the company's stock brought Graham into direct negotiations with the Gillette Company in early 1978 when plans for the purchase of Liquid Paper were initiated. The sale of Liquid Paper Company to Gillette for $47.5 million was final in October 1979. Graham sees the sale as a solution that "will reinstate the royalty contract so that the Bette Clair McMurray Foundation will again have funds to work with, and that pleases me."

Bette Graham says that women must avoid emotional decisions like hers when they enter business. She cautions that "women must learn to fight, but to fight with love. They must become more aggressive, and by that, I mean more confident of their abilities."

Bette Graham died on May 12, 1980, during preparation of this book.

Mary Grigsby

The night before her only child was to leave for college, Mary Grigsby worked at her office until nearly midnight. But the next morning she entered the kitchen early and cooked all day and into the evening, for she wanted to send along enough food to guarantee a few weeks of good nutrition for her departing son. Grigsby is a no-nonsense woman who has probably not wasted more than twenty-four hours in the last twenty-four years. Thirty years after she joined Houston First Savings and Loan Association as a bookkeeper, she became president of the company. In late 1979, Houston First merged with American Savings to form Houston First American Savings Association with assets of $1.2 billion and thirty-two offices.

Grigsby didn't plan, as a child, to grow up and become a financial expert or corporate president, but she does remember always possessing a competitive streak. "I wanted to be the best at everything, even jumping rope." She attended Western Reserve University in Cleveland, where she grew up, and after her parents moved to Colorado, she studied at Denver University. Although she never received a degree, soon after she joined Houston First, she began attending courses offered by the American Savings and Loan Institute. "No one urged me to take the classes, but I've taken nearly everything the Institute offers that I thought would help me," she says.

Grigsby has a folksy quality, a down-home sense of humor that reflects the Ohio, Colorado and Texas influences in her life. She is a confident woman who assumed no pretensions during her corporate climb to the top. Unless Grigsby thinks publicity will benefit her company, she shuns the limelight. "I don't have time for fooling around," she explains. Her work is a paramount concern, and pleasure, for her, and when she talks business, she is all business.

Initially cool and slightly aloof, she becomes affable during later meetings. Only a hint of executive reserve remains as she talks about her avocations, her love of a good poker or bridge game, her choices for the best bass-fishing spots in the state. She refers often and affectionately to her husband, crediting him with wholehearted support of her work. "With everything from putting a potato in the oven for dinner to understanding if I have to work real late, my husband is behind me," she exclaims.

Her own philosophy of decision making—work your hardest, consider all alternatives, make your decision, then don't worry over what you cannot control—crystallized soon after she married Robert Grigsby. "I was engaged to another boy and met my husband and, after just a few dates, married him. I was visiting my mother and I was all upset. I wondered if I had done the right thing and I was going on and on. My mother was preparing dinner. She stopped and looked at me and all she said was, 'If it works, it works. If it doesn't work, it doesn't work. What the heck. Let's eat.'"

After Grigsby arrived in Houston with her husband, she found that she was making no friends on her own. "Everyone I knew was someone my husband knew through his work or friendships. I had worked before I married and I just wasn't the type to do volunteer work, so I decided to get a job. I found three jobs in one day." She chose the job with Houston First, she says, "only because it was near my husband's job and we could ride to work together."

Soon after she joined the company, World War II called many of the male employees into the service. "I'm sure that I got some promotions because many of the men were gone. But I always worked long and did my job. I'd stay until two or three in the morning on big projects." She was later transferred to the loan-closing department and became a loan officer in 1945. During the next twenty years, Grigsby progressed steadily from assistant secretary to secretary, vice-president, executive vice-president. She remembers vividly when W. E. Dyche, Jr., was named president of the company and chose her as executive vice-president. "Mr. Dyche told me, 'I want to let you know that when I step down as president, you will probably be out of a job, because usually a president gets his pick for executive vice-president, and there's just no way that we can make a woman president.'" Grigsby accepted that fact, and the job, with no resentment.

But a few years later in 1971, Dyche became chairman of the board, and Grigsby was chosen president. "He tells the story that they ran an ad in the *Wall Street Journal* to find a president and that all the

54

answers came to our post office box and I threw them away," Grigsby chuckles. What really happened, she says, is that she was asked to outline the president's responsibilities. When she completed the assignment, she was asked if she could do those things. "I said yes," she says emphatically. "But I almost didn't take the job. I didn't know whether it would be good or bad for the Association because I was a woman. I knew I wanted it, and I knew if anyone else got it, I would be as mad as could be. I finally said, after a lot of debate, 'This is stupid. I want the job; I can do the job.' And I took it.''

Grigsby provoked criticism from some feminists when she discouraged female employees from wearing pantsuits until the mid-1970's, and she has refused all invitations to associate with any organized woman's groups. "I'm not for or against the woman's movement. But it seems to me, if you've got what it takes and are willing to work for what you want, you'll get it. Women who do not give the time, energy or concentration to a job that a man does cannot be treated as equals. But women who want the responsibility and are willing to work can offer a great deal in the financial area.''

Her knowledge of the home building market earned her a place on a special Department of Housing and Urban Development task force to study housing costs and spiraling prices in 1977. "The members were from related, but different, fields, and we met many times to discuss what we could do to bring down the price of housing. We always came back to the fact that government regulation was costing more than any other factor.'' Grigsby thinks economic opportunities, both individual and corporate, are greater in Texas than in any other place in the country, even during recessionary periods. "Texas is the bright spot in the whole nation . . . . there's an attitude of enthusiasm, a dynamic feeling that is like no place else. When I got off the airplane for the first time in Texas, I could feel the electricity, the emotional energy.''

Except for the three weeks she took off from work before her son Scott was born, Grigsby has been at her job. "Not everyone can live this sort of life. You can't do it if you have a very demanding family. Hours cannot mean anything to you in a job like mine. And you have to have energy. Without stamina, you simply cannot make it.'' She appears to have an oversupply. "I don't need a lot of sleep. I go to bed around ten o'clock and watch the news and a little of Johnny Carson's monologue. Then I doze off for a while and I wake up and watch the last of Carson and most of the Tom Snyder Show. Then I go to sleep again. But there's a fishing program on the radio at 4 o'clock, so I get up and listen to that. Then I may go back to sleep for an hour, or I may get up for the day. I just have a lot of energy,'' she says.

Shelby Hearon

At one time, Shelby Hearon was married, living in an expensive Austin neighborhood, driving in carpools, active in volunteer work. During those years she began to sense a frustrating fragmentation that led her to write. ''Before I began the first book,'' she says, ''I was role playing too much of the time, like ALL the time, so that I had a very strong sense of fragmentation. I was Betty Crocker in the kitchen and Bridget Bardot in the bedroom and Maria Montessori in the nursery. I was trying to remember what it had felt like to feel like one person. 'Where had Shelby gone?' I didn't think I'd seen her since she was nine, which is a long time to go back.

''I was trying to remember and to get again what it felt like to not be able to wait to get up in the morning. Just to leap out of bed 'cause you just couldn't wait to get up. I wanted that again. So I thought 'What is it that I actually do, as opposed to what I say or think I want to do.' And I had always kept a journal. I had always written, I had just never planned on being a writer. I had written in school, and you just write all the time when you're in school. I think I missed that more than I realized. I thought about that and thought about the journal. And I thought that I didn't know how I felt until I saw what I said in my journal and that I used the journal for reality testing.''

Hearon began writing her first novel, *Armadillo in the Grass,* when her younger child entered school. The book was five years under her pen. A first draft was completely thrown away, and from ten pages salvaged from her second draft, she constructed the final manuscript.

"Because the overriding theme in my life is trouble with reality, it was very important to me to get the manuscript to the point where, if I thought it was good, a publisher would think it was good. A great air of unreality hangs about would-be writers which I hate. I heard a lot of 'You have to have connections in New York to get published,' or 'They don't really appreciate good stuff when they see it.' I think if two publishers say 'It isn't good,' then it isn't good.

"I was about thirty-two when I began *Armadillo,* and I thought that if I was not published by the time I was forty, if I wasn't making it as a writer, that I would go into counseling. That's because it is the other field that people who can't communicate go into," she says. Her manuscript was immediately accepted by Alfred Knopf for publication, and by the time it appeared on the bookstands in 1968, Hearon was serving as president of the Austin Junior League and had her second novel under way.

Her League work she says gave her a sense of community. "I knew I didn't want to spend my life doing good, yet I had some sort of vague feeling that I needed to do something for the community, and for the hours I put in, I could make more change working with the League on projects than licking envelopes at the Democratic headquarters. Rather than fragmentation, it was a tie to the community."

Hearon has encountered differing reactions to her League work among feminist groups. "The League thing is very interesting, because when I speak to really radical lesbian feminists, the age 20 groups, . . . they understand power and the use of power and why you do that and what you're getting out of it. I've spoken at other groups where people will say, 'I've never allowed myself to read your books because you were a member of the Junior League.' They're putting a barrier against me because, if I'm a writer, I have to fit into the box they imagine for me. The more radical the group, the more they understand that you don't have to fit into typical images, that writers are camouflaged in one way or another."

Hearon did not spend years dreaming of becoming a writer. "I never planned to write and I still don't PLAN to write. I just write. Writing is a kind of ongoing therapy for me . . . I'm moving, say, from my problem with my mother to some general things about family pathology to the idea that things are not what they seem, reality and all that. This is what's going on below the surface in my own life in the therapy sense. So when I'm starting a book, I'm starting where I am in that sense. My books are always ahead of where I am. In *Hannah's House* the daughter gets married at nineteen. At the time I wrote it, my daughter was at Sarah Lawrence, getting ready to transfer to Columbia. But she got married the day she turned twenty. I must have known on some level that was coming. And I think I was trying out being single in fiction before I tried it in reality.''

Hearon was divorced after her fourth novel, *Now and Another Time,* was written. ''My husband didn't read my books, so I felt that I had to be single because that was driving me crazy. I don't think one has to be single to write. But in my case, it was just that I was dealing with someone who had been my friend for years. We did fine when we were dealing with his life, and not very well when we were dealing with mine. He did not want to deal with the fact that more of me was in the books than in his bed. I think he was afraid of dealing with the fact that we were not one and the same person, which he was going to find out if he read the books.

''In *Now and Another Time* I had been saying that everybody lives on the dreams of their parents. Everybody acts parts in plays they have read. And that seemed, and is, a very depressing message. When I began *A Prince of a Fellow* I was thinking, 'But some of us do become authentic. Some of us do learn to act and not react. Some of us do take hold of our lives. How do we do that?' which is how that book started.''

Hearon draws little from the personal journal, which she still keeps, for her fiction. ''My journal is really writing to myself, where I can really just level with myself and not write, even secretly, for my grandchildren to see some day. Now, for my fiction, I keep notes and folders with scraps of conversations. I steal all the time. People say things or do things that I write down and keep all tucked away,'' she says. Before writing *A Prince of a Fellow,* Hearon spent nearly six months in New Braunfels, the Texas town on which her fictional Germanic community was based. ''I had to find out what was reasonable, what could happen there, before I could write the story. All I knew when I began my research was that she [the central character] was going to survive, she was going to make it.''

All of Hearon's published writing has been set in Texas, and she has no objection to being considered a Texas or a regional writer. ''I like it very much. It never hurts me to hear that. I think books have to be set somewhere.'' Hearon was born in Marion, Kentucky, the oldest of four daughters; her father, a geologist, moved the family to Texas during her childhood, then moved them back to Kentucky. ''It's not as orderly as it may sound. I went to dozens of schools, two years in boarding school in Louisville when my hometown school was no longer college preparatory. But my family moved back to Austin when I was sixteen in 1947, and I have been there since.

''I think the fact that Texas is very in right now in New York has helped me with my agent and editors. But I don't think readers in Omaha care that a story is set in Texas, they just care that it is set some place. I mean, Texas is a million different places. But, it's become a myth like Mississippi became a myth. The same things could have happened in Alabama, things as valid, as real, as translatable. But Mississippi became a myth. And I think it's the same thing Texas represents. It stands for something.'' Hearon contributes occasionally to magazines, but she says, ''It's for the money. And also, they love it in New York that they love you in *Texas Monthly.*''

After publishing five novels, Hearon helped former Congresswoman Barbara Jordan write her autobiography. Hearon describes the experience of working with Jordan as ''Wonderful! Just wonderful. I didn't want to do the book and she didn't want to do the book. But after the first night, when I talked to her, it was okay.'' Hearon says she did no research prior to taping conversations with Jordan. She only read the King James version of the Bible, because, she says, ''Barbara Jordan speaks in Old Testament syntax and I wanted to be prepared for that.'' After the interviews, Hearon spent time with Jordan's family, teachers, colleagues and friends, studied Jordan's scrapbook, and went to Washington to consult other primary sources. ''I didn't want to prejudge what I heard from her based on what I had read from secondary sources. I didn't want that, because I thought, without realizing it, I would be asking questions that would set things up or I would be excluding other possibilities. I did all the research after taping her.''

Although pleased with the results of this effort, Hearon has no intention of writing other nonfictional books like the Jordan work. ''I just don't think I would find anybody else like that. She's just wonderful. But if you have ever dealt with anyone who has an ego, you know that collaboration can be HORRIBLE, HORRIBLE. I wouldn't have taken that book if I had seen she was that way.''

In 1977, Hearon moved into a new, sparsely furnished stone house in a subdivision of ranchettes with acreage outside Austin. The interior of the house is subdued, painted and furnished with grey tones. At the top of the stairs is her office, with its clutter of white paper and yellow legal pads, bookcases filled with bright bindings, quotations thumbtacked haphazardly to walls and spilling onto shelves. It is here that she completed her work on the Jordan book and here that, as the 1980's begin, she is working on her sixth novel.

Hearon looks, moves and dresses younger than she is. She nestles into the wooden rocker on the porch, comfortable in her blue jeans and denim shirt and, as she talks, runs shortnailed fingers through her newly frizzed hair. ''All reviews are good reviews . . . I loved having my picture in *Newsweek* and I like all the reviews. When Larry

McMurtry says about *Now and Another Time* all these things about me and Thackeray, I know he is sitting at his typewriter, looking at all his books and thinking, 'I've got to compare it to something ,'" she says laughing at the image in her mind.

But Hearon answers more thoughtfully when asked how she would judge the success of one of her novels. "I would decide it was successful if it was in a book club and making lots of money, but short of that . . . I mean, that's one kind of success. But short of that, you want to be read. And when somebody calls and says your paperback is in the Omaha Airport, that's success too."

Gladys Heldman

To say that Gladys Heldman is energetic is to say that Texas is warm in the summer. It's just not enough. Her tennis history, her publishing experience, her novel, her efforts to place qualified women on the boards of major corporations, even her self-taught foreign languages, all attest that the mind which rests—or rather, never rests—inside her lean, athletic body tosses ideas faster than a ball machine set on high speed.

Heldman is an efficient, disciplined woman. Once an idea has caught her fancy, she completely devotes herself to its fulfillment. She has a miser's regard for minutes and speaks despairingly of friends who spend too much time on unnecessary doctor's visits or too much energy trying to maintain youthful countenances. "I wear sunglasses all the time so I won't have to get an eye job," she claims, refusing to remove her sunglasses for photographs. She is not one to sit and casually read magazines while waiting for an appointment herself. For years, crossword puzzles filled those odd moments, until she realized how much of her time they had consumed. Then with the zeal that a law student spends preparing for the bar exams, she began studying Japanese in her spare time.

There is nothing self-effacing about Gladys Heldman: She will willingly demonstrate her tennis serve, point to the books she has written about tennis or speak a few words of Japanese. Yet her wry sense of humor and obvious enthusiasm for her projects prevent her from appearing arrogant.

"How did I raise my girls and do all I did?" she repeats the inquiry. "I just ignored them," she laughs. Later, however, she fondly describes how her two young daughters worked beside her as she put together issues of the tennis magazine that she founded in the early 1950's.

Because her low, husky voice is more eastern in its accent when she grows sarcastic, she often sounds as though she just arrived from La Guardia Airport. Her father was New York lawyer and jurist George Z. Medalie. Her mother—a globetrotter who went to Africa for safaris, to India for a look at the small towns, and repeatedly to France where she never stayed in the same hotel twice—studied politics at Oxford when she was seventy-nine. Heldman was raised in a family that encouraged curiosity, achievement and the efficient use of time.

Gladys Heldman graduated first in her class at Stanford University in 1942 with a degree in medieval history and took her masters the following year while teaching calculus and differential equations at the Williams Institute in Berkeley—a feat she accomplished without having studied first-year math. And she LOVES to tell the story that, in spite of these credentials, when she applied for a job, she was asked if she could type. "No, well then you'll have to be a receptionist instead of a secretary," she was told. Less than thirty years later, she sold her successful magazine, *World Tennis,* for $2,150,000.

Heldman is a two-time Texan. She lived in the state during the early 1950's but moved to New York when her husband was transferred there. The couple returned to Houston in 1970, to a contemporary home with a frequently used tennis court only steps from the back door. During the intervening years, she helped bring tennis from the seclusion of manicured country club courts to the attention of the general public.

Heldman never played tennis until her marriage, the day after her college graduation, to Julius Heldman who had played well on the amateur circuit as a teenager and later won several national senior single championships. Although Gladys Heldman was a latecomer to tennis, once she began playing, she often played three sets before, sometimes instead of, every meal. During the early 1950's, she was the top-ranked women's player in Texas, and in 1954 she played at Wimbledon, losing 6–0, 6–0, far from center court. Later, as a senior player, Heldman maintained her top-ranking, both in singles and, teamed with her daughter Julie, in the mother-daughter doubles.

It is not, however, as a competitor—feisty though she may be when playing—that Gladys Heldman has made her mark on tennis. Rather, as the editor and publisher of *World Tennis,* she stimulated discussion about the problems of the game and helped to promote tennis as a major spectator and participation sport in the United States. Starting as a single-page, mimeographed handout ''The Houston Tennis News'' in 1950, her magazine not only encouraged tennis professionals but also brought the sport to the attention of amateur players and potential players, many of them women who had never participated in competitive athletics.

In 1959, when the United States Lawn Tennis Association (later U. S. T. A.) voted not to hold the 56th installment of the indoor nationals, Heldman guaranteed the promoters against loss. The never-before-profitable tournament netted $8,000 under her guidance. She also tried to broaden international participation in tennis by airlifting gifted amateurs from around the globe to American tournaments, finding them bed and board and willing sponsors.

In the pages of *World Tennis* and elsewhere, Heldman fought fiercely and consistently for the fair treatment of all players, particularly of women. In 1970 she became the mother of the Women's Pro Tour when women players, finally rebelling against the discrepancy in prize monies offered to men and women, threatened to boycott major tournaments. After efforts to negotiate an increase in prize money for women at the 1970 U. S. Open failed, Heldman speedily arranged a tournament at the Houston Racquet Club for eight members of the dissident group. The tournament raised $7,500 in prize money: $5,000 from the sale of tickets and the remainder from the Phillip Morris Company, manufacturer of Virginia Slims cigarettes, which later with Heldman's direction established the Virginia Slims Circuit. On the second day of the unauthorized tournament, the participants received telegrams stating that they were suspended from the U. S. L. T. A. Although the official tennis establishment continued to impose various suspensions for some time, Heldman candidly observes, ''When you can talk money, no one gives a damn about suspension. Besides how can all the men in the world suspend all the women in the world!''

Heldman kept up her battle with the officials on the U. S. T. A. for more women's professional tournaments and larger purses. To establish peace between the U. S. T. A. and the Women's Pro Tour, Heldman agreed to leave her position with the Virginia Slims Circuit in 1973. ''It worked out for the best. The U. S. T. A. had tried to prevent women from playing in organized professional women's tournaments. In 1973 they agreed they would no longer fight the Women's Pro Tour. The fight was over,'' she says. In 1978 when the Virginia Slims tournaments finally crumbled, Heldman brought the Avon Company, already involved in tennis through the sponsoring of a futures circuit for lesser-ranked players, into the scene, and the Avon Championship Tournament for women was established.

Heldman received much praise, and equally as much criticism, for her staunch support of transsexual Renee Richards' right to compete with the women. When members of the Women's Tennis Association said they would boycott a Hawaiian tournament in late 1976 because of Richards' entry, Heldman stood up in the meeting and announced, "Fine. I'll play and my women friends from Houston will play. And I'll come in second and get $4,500 a week. Goodby." The W.T.A. members went to Hawaii and played in the tournament.

"I fought for Renee Richards and that wasn't popular," Heldman says. "One of my corporate clients didn't like it and it probably cost me a fair amount of money to do it. But if I hadn't fought for her, I'd probably have on my tombstone, 'Gladys kept silent about Renee Richards, because it might have cost her a fee.'"

By the time competition for press time and paper convinced her to sell *World Tennis,* Heldman had come a long way from the days of answering the telephone with one voice, saying "One moment, please," then changing her voice to become the advertising chief or distribution clerk or editor the caller had requested. She signed a five-year contract, later renewed, with the magazine's new owners to contribute articles on a regular basis.

After selling her magazine in 1972, Heldman established Gladys Heldman and Associates, which tried to place women on the boards of major corporations across the country. Heldman claims that in a period of five years she located and placed qualified women on the boards of many of the country's fifty top banks and major industrial firms. An outspoken feminist, Heldman once persuaded both Gloria Steinem and Bobby Riggs to appear on the same podium to raise money for the National Women's Political Caucus.

As for women's tennis, Heldman says, "I don't ever want to get back into women's professional tennis again. One changes. I'd much rather do a celebrity tournament in Japan with Burt Bacharach. Or work with Pancho Segura and Pancho Gonzales arranging fun tournaments. I'm happy. Arranging father and son doubles tournaments, celebrity events, women's senior contests . . . there's not as much strain. I've had enough fights to last me a while."

By the mid-1970's, Heldman's energies were trained on a new project, writing a novel, which had been in the back court of her mind for nearly thirty years. "Everyone wants to write a novel, but few people really believe they'll ever do it. I certainly didn't. I would think about it occasionally, but I never had a theme. Then, when the theme came, I got to work on developing the plot and characters. It was a lot of hard work, but it was fun. If you really decide you want to do something, whether it's learn to play tennis or write a novel, the fun is in giving it endless hours of effort, in being anxious to go to bed at night because you can't wait to get back to the work in the morning. That's how it was writing the book. It was enthralling.'' The result, *The Harmonetics Investigation,* published in late 1979, examines the attraction of and devotion to cult-type religious groups, while drawing from her diverse interests and opinions: publishing, tennis, Japan, the national quest for youth, the medical profession. Heldman enjoyed preparing the book more than promoting it. Time spent taping interviews for replay on a remote radio station's 4:00 A.M. farm program was not well spent, she says.

Heldman's many interests have made her popular on the lecture circuit, and since 1977, she has lectured as a Fellow for the Woodrow Wilson National Fellowship Foundation. Although she would prefer lecturing on philosophy, logic, and semantics—mental exercises have always intrigued her—she receives more requests for less weighty subjects that reflect her own experiences: publishing, the equality of the sexes, writing a novel, the influence of western culture on Japanese women, and tennis. And she did all of this without ever learning to type.

Joanne Herring

On cue, as though a stage director had shouted "Roll 'em!" the tall French doors swing open and through them enters Joanne Herring. There is something special about meeting Joanne King Herring—an impression that you are both witness to and participant in a theatrical performance, and there's no question about who gets top billing. Her covergirl face and trim figure are those of a star. The voice, as smooth as good cream gravy, rises dramatically to emphasize a point. The end of a thought is punctuated with a pursing of full lips and a widening of brilliant blue eyes.

As Joanne Johnson, flashing a "show biz" personality that remains her trademark, she was first runner-up to the Sweetheart of the University when she attended the University of Texas. It was a disappointment, not winning, but her father consoled her with the old saw: "It's when they stop talking about you that you've got to worry."

And they haven't stopped talking. Seen jogging in *People* magazine, pronounced one of the elite "In" people by fashion writers, quoted in syndicated columns on subjects ranging from flirting to her personal war against communism, or profiled in the *Washington Post,* she has become an international "item" with a paradoxical life-style. Herring can take traditionally low-profile, even lackluster, jobs—fund raising, business, entertaining, consular positions, even exercising—and turn them into glamourous showcases. With a Hollywood aura about her, she has organized charity balls, served on the boards of theater, ballet, symphony, opera and museum groups in Houston, and led fund-raising campaigns for multiple sclerosis, muscular dystrophy, and Easter seals.

In the course of an afternoon's conversation, Joanne Herring moves from the weighty to the trivial, the momentous to the frivolous. She says, sincerely, that she once asked herself if she could be a missionary. Her answer was yes, but she also decided that Divine Providence wanted her right where she was, motioning around the handsome library of her home. Talking about the needs of women and children in developing countries, her voice falters with emotion. Then her voice moves upward as she mentions internationally famous guests who have accepted a party invitation. Later, donning a decollette evening dress and posing for photographs, she appears the quintessential femme fatale, while talking about the significant changes that women's roles in society have undergone. Although changeable, like a lovely chameleon, she also has constants: Joanne Herring is charming, enthusiastic, optimistic, patriotic, and gregarious.

She once hoped to become a film star. But the telegram announcing she had been chosen to play an Indian princess whose only on-camera line was "ugh," came the day of her wedding to Robert King. After having two children and "doing all the usual volunteer work," she became a talk show hostess for a Houston television station. "When I first started, the cameramen, the lighting people, everyone said I was terrible . . . . But the people who watched at home seemed to enjoy my guests and what we talked about . . . . Why didn't I quit when the people in the business said I was bad? Why quitting just never has been part of my makeup."

She remained a television hostess for twelve years, until 1975, was also active in producing television specials, and was named official hostess of Texas. During those years her marriage to King ended in divorce. "I remember how hard it was, trying to work and do a good job and then come home and bake cookies and play with the children . . . . It's just a shame that the time for establishing yourself in a career comes at the same time as having children and raising a family. It is really difficult for young women to do both and not be exhausted."

She is married now to Robert Herring, chairman of the board of Houston Natural Gas Company. Her parties have become legend: Royalty and officials from around the world have spread caviar at her table. Many are entertained at the request of the State Department or by the visitors' governments, but many also are friends. For the numerous visitors from the oil-rich countries, a room suggestive of Scheherazade—an elaborate concoction of floor pillows, tents, everything but sand dunes—has been created in the otherwise French rococo-furnished Herring home.

But Herring is a party girl with a purpose. "Business is why we have a party . . . . At our parties, I invite people who I think will like each other and can perhaps help each other. They are people I have sort of screened, so guards can be lowered. The evening is not all dollars and cents, but we can all work better with someone with whom we have rapport. Bob and I put together an interesting mixture. I know a lot of the so-called jet set and we put them together with Bob's business friends. Everyone is thrilled to death because it is a chance to meet and know people who are different . . . it's like a bouquet," she says, gesturing with a long, slow sweep of the hand toward a towering arrangement of fresh, exotic flowers. "If every flower were the same, it would be s-o-o-o dull."

Life is anything but dull for Herring. As honorary consul for Pakistan and for Morocco, she is the only woman in the country to hold dual consulate positions, and the first woman to represent either of the two countries in diplomatic posts. In Pakistan she has convinced government officials to organize cottage industry, producing hand-embroidered dresses and linens, for export. "The money goes to the people who made the goods, not to some wealthy Pakistani." Herring hopes the Morocco economy can be bolstered by an expansion of cottage trade and tourism. Potential plans include production of travelogue films, with Herring as hostess, to encourage travel in Morocco.

When it comes to promoting what she considers worthy causes, Herring has abundant energy, an ability to rally support and a talent for convincing her listeners that their wit is remarkable, their presence a treat. One Houston retail executive said of her, after donating more time and money to one of her charitable productions than he had planned, "She was so damned persistent, but so charming, I became committed in spite of myself. If she had been a man, I'd have sent him out of my office empty-handed."

Although Herring has roamed far from her native state, she remains at heart a Texan. "Texas is so different. Most Texans are such individuals. There is openness here. In Texas, everything depends more on what you are than who you are. If you are special, you can get into any group. Sure, it takes a certain amount of money if you want to reciprocate, but that isn't even so important. If you have something to offer, there is a place for you in Texas," she smiles.

Joanne Herring appears to enjoy the place she has carved out for herself in Texas. Corporate wife, mother, supporter of charities, television personality, international hostess, consul—it seems like an incongruous collection of roles for anyone but a woman who had considered careers as both a movie star and a missionary.

Oveta Culp Hobby

Her office, a three-room suite on the third floor of *The Houston Post* building, was moved section by section from the old *Post* headquarters downtown because she didn't want to part with it. It is a commanding room, handsomely furnished with antiques, paintings, and books. Her mahogany desk sits in a corner of glass walls, flanked by the American flag from her Women's Army Corps days and the pennant of the Department of Health, Education, and Welfare from her years as HEW Secretary. But, as Oveta Culp Hobby rises from behind her desk and extends a hand, the office might just as well be a nondescript cubicle, for she becomes the only thing in the room to observe.

Her eyes fix like epoxy to yours as she talks, then listens. Her face is expressive. A broad, toothful grin can be quickly followed by lips closed firmly, pensive and thoughtful. Her eyebrows arch as she laughs but settle into a composed line above her sharp blue eyes as she listens during questions. Her Distinguished Service Medal sits on the collar of her pastel ultrasuede dress. Her hair is tucked under a soft turban, one of the vast collection of hats that have become here trademark. She has a regal elegance that is frequently democratized by a hearty laugh. The chairman of the board and editor of *The Houston Post,* Hobby has that quality often called presence, a quality she has exuded since childhood.

Born the second child in a family of six children in Killeen, Texas, in 1905, Hobby was given the Cherokee name Oveta, which her mother had read in a romantic novel and liked. It has, she says, been misspelled and mispronounced all her life. Her father, Isaac Culp, was a

Bell County attorney and politician who served in the state legislature. As a child, Oveta Culp shared her father's interest in politics and would go to Austin when he was in the legislature for brief visits. She helped her father in his Killeen office and would stop by after school, "just to see if there was anything I could do." Before she was ten, Oveta was reading the *Congressional Record*. "Living in a small town as I did . . . . I guess the Congressional Record was sort of spectacular in that it had very broad horizons . . . . It touched all parts of the world, all kinds of issues, and it was an interesting document. Still is, as a matter of fact."

Her father, along with her husband, are those she cites when she talks about the major motivating forces in her life. "My father expected a lot of me. He was the one who always kept after me to do my best. Certainly my mother and father didn't categorize what was for a girl and what was for a boy to do."

Her mother, Emma Hoover Culp, though busy with home, children, gardening and civic work, was also active politically. "We had an enormous orchard with peaches, plums and pears. I spent weeks canning fruit in 1918 while my mother went out campaigning for William Hobby [Oveta Culp's future husband] in his race for governor. That was the first year that women were voting. [Hobby] had gotten that bill through the legislature so women could vote that year . . . . My mother and a great many other women I knew were really out in the hustings looking for votes for him."

Her mother's influence remains in other slight ways. While Hobby frequently draws a cigarette from her red leather, gold-initialed box, she pushes it away during photographs, laughing, "I still think of what my mother would say if she saw me smoking."

Life was not all *Congressional Record* and canning. Oveta Culp Hobby remembers playing chase with friends: While some pretended to be Ku Klux Klan members, the rest ran after them in a politically aware version of cowboys and Indians. An avid reader even then, she remembers her father "always complaining about my sister's clothing bills and my book bills." Active in theatrical performances, at one time during childhood she thought she might become an actress. She continued in community theater during her young married years. "I love the theater. I'd still take part if I had the time," she says now.

Hobby graduated from Temple High School and enrolled at Mary Hardin-Baylor College but left college after one year for Austin where she audited a few law courses. At the age of twenty she was appointed the first woman parliamentarian of the Texas House of Representatives, a job she returned to in 1931, 1939 and 1941. By 1928, as a legal clerk in the state banking department she had codified the state banking laws. In 1929 she worked as an assistant to Houston City

74

Attorney John H. Freeman, and the next year, she lost a close race for the state legislature. Houston had become her home base, and when a job was offered in the circulation department of the *Post,* she took it.

After serving as governor, William Hobby had returned to the *Post* and was president of the company when Oveta Culp came to work there. Following a courtship of several months, William Hobby, 55, and Oveta Culp, 26, were married in 1931. But the Culp was never dropped from her name. ''My husband laughed once and said, 'No matter what you do, or what titles you've had from time to time, no one ever calls you anything but Oveta Culp Hobby.' I've never understood it myself,'' she says.

During the next four years, her children (William Pettus Hobby, Jr., and Jessica Hobby) were born. While awaiting the birth of her daughter, she wrote a textbook on parliamentary procedure, *Mr. Chairman,* based on her experience in the Texas legislature and as president of the Texas League of Women Voters. She continued to work at the *Post,* writing a series of articles on community issues. Hobby also was active in the symphony society and in fund raising for the University of Houston and was appointed to a state committee that sought appropriations for needy, blind or dependent children.

She shakes her head in immediate dissent when asked how she reconciled working with the guilt that many young working mothers feel at leaving young children. ''Guilt connotes criminality. I don't think it is a sense of guilt as much as a sense of regret, of dissatisfaction at being unable to be in two places at once. And I don't think that feeling is restricted to women. I am sure men must feel regret when they cannot spend as much time with their children as they would wish. So I think people use the wrong word when they use guilt. At any critical time in my family's life, I have always been with them, . . . so there is no question about where the first comes, no question.''

In 1939, friend Jesse Jones, who had controlling ownership in both the *Post* and *The Houston Chronicle,* decided to sell the *Post.* The Hobbys purchased *The Houston Post* for $4 million and continued working as a team in adjoining offices. Although the *Post* had been operating in the red, it soon became profitable; the Hobby media empire is now valued conservatively at more than $200 million.

A year later, Oveta Culp Hobby was chosen by Franklin Roosevelt to head the women's section of the War Department's Bureau of Public Relations. Her appointment came despite her opposition to a third term for Roosevelt ''as a matter of principal,'' although she ''liked Mrs. Roosevelt and President Roosevelt very much.'' When the Women's Army Auxiliary Corps was created in 1942, Hobby was put in charge. She recalls, ''During the formation of the WAAC, there

was the feeling that women in uniform in the service were not needed
. . . . When it became apparent that the war would be fought on two fronts, and military personnel would be needed in greater numbers, there was growing acceptance.''

Hobby traveled across the country recruiting officer candidates and to England with Mrs. Roosevelt to study the war work of British women. ''Hand me my sword!'' she would exclaim when she left her office at the Pentagon for congressional meetings. During the first weeks, when hers was the first and only uniform, she washed out her uniform at night and ironed it herself before speaking engagements the next morning. The hard-brimmed hat she wore around the world was flattering and came to be known as the Hobby hat, ''but it was not designed for me and I was not the sole person who selected that hat,'' Hobby laughs now. When the ''Auxiliary'' was dropped from the WAAC, Hobby became a colonel, and by the time she resigned her post in 1945, the original congressional list of 54 jobs suitable for women had been stretched by Hobby to 239, and members of the WAC were working as riveters, interpreters, balloon-gas chemists, surveyors and boiler inspectors in such far-flung places as India, North Africa and Egypt.

''I think women working during the war had a tremendous influence on moving women into the labor force—not only those who served in the military, but also those who held jobs in the factories and other war-related jobs. When I went to say goodbye to General Marshall when I left, he said, 'When you're rested, write a memorandum to the file on utilization of women power . . . .' I smiled at him and I said 'General, I'll write it if you tell me to, but if you need to recruit women in such numbers again, the conditions will be different! You have no idea what is going to happen in the woman power field as a result of this war, because of women in the armed services and in the civilian jobs that they took during the war.' ''

Oveta Culp Hobby was awarded the Distinguished Service Medal in 1945, the first woman to receive that award; little more than thirty years later she received the Marshall Medal for Public Service, the highest award given by the Association of the United States Army. Hobby was the nineteenth recipient and the first woman to receive that award.

As a reporter for the *Post*, Hobby covered Security Council meetings of the fledgling United Nations during 1946. Although very active in publishing (she served in 1949 as president of the Southern Newspaper Publishers Association), her political activities continued as well. She helped convince presidential candidate Tom Dewey to support state ownership of the Tidelands in 1948. Later she led the

National Citizens for Eisenhower organization. After his election, Oveta Culp Hobby was appointed Federal Security Agency Administrator, responsible for a department with 35,000 employees, administrative offices in Washington and ten regional offices. The Office of Education, the Office of Vocational Rehabilitation and the Social Security Administration were all under her jurisdiction.

When the FSA was reorganized in 1953 and became the Department of Health, Education and Welfare, Oveta Culp Hobby was appointed its first Secretary. She looks at contemporary problems within the department with an eye toward the bottom line. "If they had done it wisely, this almost crisis need not have occurred. You have to balance when you add a benefit . . . . You go to Congress and seek additional tax money to pay for these things, or you're just like any other budget, you get out of whack. And that's exactly what's happened to it. When I was there, we increased the taxes, had a true audit, and we had about fifty of the best actuaries in the country studying that system, and we put it back on track." During her tenure as Secretary of HEW, benefits were extended to the self-employed. "We made some great improvements, but all these changes that have proved so enormously expensive and have not been put in the tax responsibility, you know, have come later, and you have to do the two together to keep it solvent."

Her husband's health began to fail in 1955 and she resigned her position and returned to Houston, assuming increasing responsibility for management of the *Post* and the KPRC radio and television stations, which the Hobbys had acquired in 1950. After her husband died in 1964, her son returned to Houston and worked with his mother until 1972 when he ran a successful campaign for lieutenant governor. Daughter Jessica, after writing for San Antonio newspapers, married diplomat Henry Catto. Jessica Catto has worked recently with former Secretary of State Henry Kissinger on his memoirs. "My daughter writes beautifully, her mother says modestly," Oveta Culp Hobby boasts with a laugh. "I saw Henry not long ago and he told me, 'I've written two thousand pages without a single verb. Jessica's going to have a problem.' "

Her paper is delivered by a toss to the sidewalk as it is to other subscribers in her River Oaks neighborhood, and Hobby is up by seven, reading the *Post* over decaffeinated coffee. She calls her office for messages, and leaves with her chauffeur for the office by nine-thirty. When she departs in the late afternoon, a thick stack of paperwork goes home with her, for study, thought and reflection. And in-between, she has attended meetings with editors, general counsel and KPRC executives, dealt with volumes of mail and kept a log full of appointments.

While Hobby often suggests story ideas at editorial sessions, she leaves day-to-day management of the *Post* to people she has chosen for that job. Hobby says the "proper role for journalism today is to inform the citizens as fully and as accurately as it is possible to do . . . . The nature of journalism has changed. You have more and more specialists. A reporter used to go out and get a story and come in and write it and that was the end of it. Well, it isn't that way anymore. You have a task force trying to get a story, and you may see a by-line with two names on it. If the truth were known, on some of these series, we've had as many as four or five people working at one story over a long period of time."

When her likeness graced the cover of *Time* magazine in 1954, Hobby was described in the long cover story as a woman "brisk without bustle." It is a description that holds true today. People who have served on committees she has chaired in the past still talk with awe-struck tones of her skill at conducting business and managing people. One Houston businessman who sat around her conference table a few years ago says, ". . . when Oveta Culp Hobby ran the committee meeting, it was like watching a puppet show. She'd pull the strings and you'd have your chance to speak. When it was over, everyone felt he had really contributed, felt he had made the meeting run smoothly. But it was really Oveta. She was gracious, attentive and soft-spoken, but she never let the meeting break down into small talk, never let it get out of her control."

Although Hobby has long been friends with many local and national newsmakers, she says that "has never interfered with my objectivity. I don't believe you'd find anyone who would say that. I'm a very lucky lady. I have never had a friend try to impose on friendship, because they know what our standards are, and they know it's news we write. I get a lot of heartache out of it, of course, when I read stories about my friends. But then, it's our business to print the news."

More than simply news, Oveta Culp Hobby wants thorough information: Her curiosity for knowledge seems never to rest. "I've never had a dull day in my life that I remember. There's always been something more I had to learn, something more I had to do," she says. When in 1977 she had read all she could find on the beginnings of the Islamic empire, she was dissatisfied and ordered a series of stories on the subject from the Associated Press. When she heard a vague discussion of the Arab Emirates, she felt she needed to know more about them and ordered a series of articles. "As the world grows smaller, we simply have to keep knowing more and more. Good decisions must be based on good information." If she hears a word in conversation that she does not use in her speaking vocabulary, she is unsatisfied until she has found the word in her dictionary, assimilated its meaning and is ready to use it in her own conversation. She remains, at heart, a student.

As photographs are taken, Hobby relaxes, unintimidated by the camera lens. She brings the session to an unrushed, lingering close.

"It is true, I was the first woman to do several jobs that were once open only to men . . . . It annoys me a little that people pull back and say, 'Well, a woman did that.' Why not a woman? I think we ought to get this out of the whole lexicon of thinking and writing, that surprise when a woman does something," she says, and pauses a moment before her hearty laugh erupts.

"You know, I was just thinking," she says, as her laughter ebbs, "men would come in my office, reporters, and they'd always look for that 'feminine touch' . . . and ask things like 'Do you know how to make hollandaise sauce?' It just throws you off. A friend of mine became president of Lord & Taylor, and I think she was the first woman head of a really big retail chain. I wired her and said right on or the equivalent that we said then, and she wrote me back and said, 'You know, Oveta, during the war, I used to read the press on you and think, *she* ought to do better than that. Then at my first big press conference, a male reporter raised his hand and asked me what size shoe I wore. I finally realized, it's out of your control. They are going to get back to the woman thing,'" Hobby recalls, adding, "I'd like to live long enough to see people not be surprised by the fact that a woman succeeded in something."

Dorothy Hood

Gray Houston skies seem to enter through the screen door and sweep into the corners of her studio-home. A plump white cat—Tosca when the artist is in one mood, Paganini when she is in another—nestles onto a floor mat. Carpet scraps are placed around the living room, providing a resting place for huge canvases. There is an intimacy between the cans holding brushes, the twisted and empty tubes of paint, and the woman who placed them all on the scarred table by the open window.

An enigmatic woman, Dorothy Hood has devoted her life to painting. Although her works have been termed ''psychic landscapes'' by critics and collectors, she rarely attempts to interpret what her paintings say for her. ''If it could be said, there would be no reason to paint it,'' she says. Her large brown eyes appear to look past exteriors, deep into thoughts. She often runs her long pale fingers through her auburn hair as she searches for words to express herself. What she can express abstractly in her art is less easily understood as she speaks.

''I read a quotation when I was young. I've tried to paint and live by it. 'Unspiritual material commotion.' I want to be the very opposite of that. I never try to reach the individual in my paintings. Message is a shallow word. I consider myself to be like everyone else, and if I reach my own psyche, then that reaching will echo to others. When I paint there is always a conflict. There is an awareness that many levels are working at the same time, like Yeats said, 'the multiplicity within the mystery.' That's the way with making a painting: the best will be that which comes from many realized directions.''

Born in Bryan, Texas, in 1919, her family moved to Houston when Hood was an infant. Her grandfather was a theater impresario; her mother, an "accomplished dilettante and powerful encourager"; her father, a banker and businessman. "I didn't have a very happy childhood . . . . Mine was very Anglo, disciplinary, Germanic. There was a lot of tension and stifling of feeling," she says.

Although not happy, she was encouraged to pursue her artistic talents and, from the age of five, knew she would be an artist. "It was the only thing I did better than anything else. My mother was far in advance of her time, and I was raised innocent of the idea that any field would be closed to me because of my sex." As a child, she often skipped her lessons at the Museum of Fine Arts, heading instead to the park or for a quiet, solitary ramble through the neighborhood. But by the time she was fourteen, she became a serious student and eventually won a scholastic scholarship to the Rhode Island School of Design, where she spent four years in study before going to New York.

Her New York days were spent frivolously "dancing 'til dawn, modeling—prancing like a horse to support myself—constant parties. I believe that all of my depth came from that period of being too intensely frivolous," she says, "and the luckiest thing I ever did was to have a bad love affair and go off to Mexico." Hood intended to spend only a few weeks in Mexico while a friend exhibited art in a show there in 1942. Instead, except for occasional trips to South America and the United States, she spent the next twenty years in Mexico.

"There were compound reasons why I stayed. The people were dignified, beautiful, but had great emotional empathy. The physical beauty of the place was overwhelming. And also, as an artist, I could see before me a great long struggle of 'how do I subsist and still go on with my art?' There was a favorable money exchange at the time, and my stipend from the family was very tiny." Hood laughs, and the sound is one produced only by bad memories turned humorous with time. "I had modeled and had all those beautiful clothes. But as my money ran low, I had to buy those rope-soled sandals to wear with the fantastic wardrobe. It rained so often; I was always wet, and I always had a cold."

Hood also felt that she was accepted more readily as an artist in Mexico than she would have been in the United States. "The artisan was so very important, and the artist was at the top of the cultural community. Even as a woman-artist, there was a certain homage that I received, a respect for the creative ability and drive." There were lucky breaks from the beginning. Poet Pablo Neruda wrote a poem about her and her work, which helped bring her to the attention of others in the art colony. She was also befriended by artist Jose Clemente Orozco. "He was a man of great integrity, very intense, and life hadn't done a thing to his ideals. All young people start out with integrity, but somehow it usually gets lost along the way.

"From the time I arrived in Mexico I was treated as an artist, not a student. I found that there was no hierarchy that I had to pass through in Mexico. Practically the whole Spanish republic was in exile there. They met in an old hotel downtown for noon dinner . . . writers, poets, artists. My studio was centrally located and they all came. I was, you must remember, only twenty-two years old. Then later, when I married [Bolivian composer Velasco Maidana] and traveled with my husband, I identified with the younger artists, Diego Rivera and Rufino Tamayo among them. I still enjoy identifying with the young. If they like a show, it tells me the work is living. The young make me free."

One of her early drawings was accepted by the Museum of Modern Art in New York, where she has paintings now. Others of her canvases are now in the permanent collections of the Museo de Art Moderno, Mexico City, and of twenty-three American museums, including the Whitney Museum of American Art, New York; the Brooklyn Museum; the Philadelphia Museum of Art; and the San Francisco Museum of Modern Art.

Her work has been described as a synthesis of many traditions; her inspirations are as complex. While her formal art study was a necessary discipline, the source of Hood's art derives from her intellectual and spiritual associations in Mexico, combined with extensive reading, reflection and study of western and oriental inquiries into the realm of the spirit. "Ideas produce art," she says. "I don't paint physical beauty, but I prefer instead to paint what is in my mind."

Hood and her husband left Mexico in the late 1960's. "Things began falling apart, the artists were in a state of mental and spiritual commotion. A malaise set in, although my work was getting better, and I felt it was time to come back to my roots." She believes that by living in Texas she is following the Taoist advice to live life, as she says, "in the fruit and not in the flower. There is a rough energy in Texas, a physical presence of energy in the oil wells, the wild driving. It is a take chance society. While I might have received more acclaim if I had lived elsewhere, I have produced a great body of my art in Texas, and I am influenced by the energy I feel here."

She muses about "the battles yet to be fought. I haven't received full recognition yet for my art. I must admit I want that. And I would like to reach a point where not only do I have something to say, but people will stop to hear it." She adds quietly, though, "You paint for the sheer joy of doing it, not for reward, or for recognition, which can come and go quickly, but for the pleasure and relief painting brings."
recognition, which can come and go quickly, but for the pleasure and relief painting brings."

Sarah T. Hughes

Young attorneys swear that if God is a woman, her face looks like Sarah Hughes.

Her once chestnut hair is highlighted with grey and white; her face is as lined as a metropolitan road map; her eyes gather water occasionally in their corners. She is a tiny woman, barely five feet tall. But there is nothing frail about her. She sits, arms folded, behind her desk, quick to question a question or rephrase an inquiry. Her answers may be as brief as those of a good witness following counsel's advice to answer only what is necessary. Then, as a surprise, she may flash a wide grin and embellish her answers, elaborate her responses. She has been called "peppery" by some who have interviewed her, "feisty" by others. But whatever she is called, U. S. District Court Judge Sarah Tilghman Hughes can reduce an uncooperative witness to tears or drive an ill-prepared attorney to tranquilizers and the nearest law library.

Her retirement from the bench was announced in 1975, when she turned seventy-nine, and articles about her read like eulogies, putting her in the past tense. But Hughes elected to remain on the bench with senior status, and she says she intends to "work until I drop over." Four and a half days a week she tries criminal cases almost exclusively, saying they are the easiest to try even though most other judges don't like to try them. The morning of her interview she rose at dawn, swam twenty lengths in the pool at her Highland Park home in Dallas and breakfasted before arriving at the courthouse, where she arraigned eleven individuals and set court dates for those entering not guilty pleas.

Hughes was appointed to the federal bench in 1961 by President John Kennedy over the protests of the attorney general that at sixty-five she was too old. Her friends, including Vice-President Lyndon Johnson, House Speaker Sam Rayburn, Senator Ralph Yarborough, and countless knowns and unknowns from the Business and Professional Women's Clubs across the country, urged her appointment.

"I believe women have to go after what they want," she says. "I'm opposed to women who constantly talk about being discriminated against. I didn't feel discriminated against in 1930. Of course, I knew that there were people who wouldn't vote for me because I was a woman. But that just made it necessary for me to work harder. I think you've got to ask for things. You can't wait to have things given to you. When I decided that I wanted to be a federal judge, I didn't think for a minute that President Kennedy would look around the State of Texas and pick me out as the most competent lawyer in the state. No! I told him about myself. I asked people if they'd do something to help me."

Hughes has been going after what she wanted since she was a Baltimore school girl whose diminutive size didn't keep her off the basketball team when she wanted to play. She attended Goucher College on an academic scholarship, graduating Phi Beta Kappa with a major in zoology and a minor in mathematics.

After teaching those subjects in high school for two years she realized that she didn't like teaching, and enrolled in night classes at George Washington University Law School. During the day she worked for the Washington, D. C., police force as one of twenty policewomen who patrolled streets, skating rinks and dance halls and investigated cases involving women and children.

Before graduation she married George Ernest Hughes, a native of Palestine, Texas, and together they moved to Dallas where he had a job waiting. Although letters and visits to almost every law firm in Dallas failed to produce a job for Sarah Hughes, two young attorneys finally permitted her to use a desk left vacant by a secretary's departure, in exchange for occasional secretarial services. Her practice grew as many of the firms that had refused her a job sent her cases they did not want to handle themselves. Her interest in politics also intensified. She stumped the state in 1928 for Alfred E. Smith and the state ticket; two years later she launched her own campaign for the state legislature.

"I'm a good campaigner," she says, "When I ran the first time I visited every small town in my district, every fire station three times because there were three shifts of men working. I went wherever there was a vote. We had speakings on the street and all the candidates spoke on the streets in small towns. And I only spent $300 for the whole campaign.''

Hughes said she began thinking of herself as a Texan the day she moved to Dallas. ''I knew I was going to live here, and by the time I was elected to the state legislature, I was accepted as a Texan . . . True,'' she laughs one of her hearty laughs with head thrown back and eyes dancing, ''True, I dug up all my ancestors to prove that I was a Southerner. There was a sheriff in Oklahoma that was a Tilghman, and there was a general in the Confederate army from Alabama. I knew that all people who have the name are related in some way, so they all became my relatives.''

She won the election and two reelection bids. During her second term she was chosen as the most valuable legislator by the newspaper capital correspondents. Her campaign platforms stressed concern for women and children, prison reform and lower taxes. ''I introduced an income tax bill . . . it didn't make me very popular, but that didn't make any difference. I felt that an income tax was the proper thing and I still feel as if it is. I'm very much opposed to a sales tax. I was able to get that income tax bill through the House [it did not pass in the Senate] and that had never been done before or since,'' she says.

Soon after the beginning of Hughes' third term, Governor James Allred appointed her judge of the 14th District Court of Texas. Her appointment raised objections from Senator Claude Westerfield from Dallas. ''He was opposed to me largely because I was a woman. But he made the mistake of announcing in the paper that I ought to be home washing dishes. Many women might not have been in favor of me being on the state court, but none of them wanted to be told that they HAD to stay in the kitchen and wash dishes.'' In addition to support from women in their kitchens, Hughes' appointment was encouraged by several Dallas women with influence in the Democratic party and by members of the Business and Professional Women's Clubs.

A photo she had taken of herself in the kitchen did not hurt her publicity.

Hughes remained a state judge until her appointment thirty years later to the federal bench, although twice she campaigned unsuccessfully for elective office. In 1946 she was defeated in a race for Congress, and in 1958 she lost her bid for the state supreme court. ''I never ran for office again because I knew I would be defeated,'' she says. ''I wouldn't have run at that time if I had known the climate in Dallas. Dallas had become extremely conservative, opposed to labor and to the things I stood for. I had made the mistake of opposing the congressman who was then in office, and made the mistake of saying I didn't like his politics. When I ran for the state supreme court, I made an excellent campaign if I do say so myself. I again made the mistake of running against an incumbent.''

In 1952, Hughes was nominated for Vice-President at the National Democratic Convention. ''That also grew out of the Business and Professional Women's Club. The New York federation had endorsed me for Vice-President and when the national Business and Professional Women's Convention came along, they offered a resolution endorsing me for Vice-President of the Democratic ticket and Margaret Chase Smith as Vice-President of the Republican . . . . Speaker Rayburn was president of the convention and he never recognized anybody unless he wanted to. So I had to get his permission to have the nomination made. First, I had to get Mr. Stevenson's permission, then Rayburn said he would permit it only if I would immediately withdraw my name.''

Exasperation roughens the edges of her voice when she is asked if, in retrospect, she should have agreed to withdraw her name. ''That was the only way I could even get nominated. The presidential candidate has the opportunity to choose his vice-presidential candidate. I knew he had chosen Senator Sparkman. If I could have been left in nomination I would have only gotten two votes, two delegates from Maine had endorsed me. I wasn't even a delegate.''

In her years on the bench, Hughes has drawn much praise and some criticism. Those who contribute to the legend around her speak of her boundless energy, quick wit, ability and determination. Her critics just as loudly condemn her endorsement of Democratic candidates while serving as a federal judge. ''As far as electioneering while I've been a judge, I admit that sometimes I go a little further than I should. But I'm still very much interested in politics,'' she says.

She has presided over cases involving obscenity, welfare, fair housing, abortion, drug possession and sales, stock fraud, civil rights. On many occasions, there is a personal touch, explaining why a particular sentence was imposed and what a defendant needs to do to get himself in better shape. She was one of three judges in the case that found Texas' laws concerning abortion unconstitutional. She heard the massive civil suit filed by the U. S. Securities and Exchange Commission in the multi-million dollar stock fraud scheme that became known as the Sharpstown Bank Scandal. She was the magistrate who ruled that the civil rights of prisoners in the Dallas county jail were violated by the inhumane conditions of the facilities. Many Dallasites call the new jail facilities 'Judge Hughes' jail.

Hughes was criticized in the mid-1970's for her decision to award probated sentences to four Dallas youths accused of selling marijuana to federal narcotics agents. The young men, all under twenty-one, pled guilty to failure to pay tax on the marijuana. But her deep-rooted conviction that in many instances a person is better rehabilitated in the community sustains her when her judgment is challenged.

Handsome landscapes on the wall of her office, photographed and framed by one of the youthful offenders, now share a place of honor in her office, along with photographs of political leaders who were friends and young law clerks who have worked with her. There is one child's photograph, of her only godchild, the daughter of a former law clerk who was later elected a congressman.

Throughout her long career, Hughes has been a supporter of equal rights for all citizens. State libraries have yellowed copies of newspaper articles, dateline 1935, in which Judge Hughes, described as "attired in a red dinner gown that accented her youth, the only woman district judge in Texas looked more like a school girl than a magistrate," urged women to take more responsibility in government. She endorsed the idea that women should be eligible for the draft more than a quarter of a century ago, and in 1952 suggested an equal rights amendment to the Constitution as well as calling for the Democratic party to endorse "equal pay for equal work." She was an early fighter for the right of women to serve on juries. She says now that no woman has a right to complain unless she votes and takes an active interest in government, and even then, Hughes recommends hard work in place of complaints.

Most of the time, Hughes takes an "objection overruled" attitude toward criticism. "I do the things I think are right. I don't have regrets. I'm like Truman. You make a decision and you don't look back. You don't have regrets for things that you can't help. You can't spend your lifetime in worrying about things you've done. You do them and you put them behind you and you go on to something else."

One thing that does raise her ire is that many people, upon hearing her name, think only of her administering the presidential oath of office to Lyndon Johnson in Dallas after President Kennedy's assassination. "That's nothing I did for myself. That's just a happenstance. I'd rather be associated with the Dallas county jail. Plenty of these cases that I've had are of some importance. I didn't do anything to swear in the President. He just happened to know me, and I had worked for him and I was the only Democratic judge around."

Lady Bird Johnson

As she walks, head up and with a pleasant smile in her eyes and on her lips, through the lobby of the Lyndon Baines Johnson Library in Austin, a wave of double takes follows her. People resting on the cushioned benches or choosing souvenirs by the cashier's stand look again, then nudge the person next to them. "It's Mrs. Johnson." "There's Lady Bird." And the murmurs pass like a Sunday collection plate through the crowd until she disappears through the front door. Outside, on the plaza overlooking the landscaped lawn she loves, she is recognized by a couple from El Campo. The woman digs through her handbag, searching for a pen, as she calls out with familiarity, "Lady Bird! Oh, Mrs. Lady Bird!" and asks for an autograph on the back of a torn grocery receipt. If Lady Bird Johnson is weary of recognition, after all her years in the public's eye, she gives no sign. Graciously, the former First Lady smiles, asks where home is, signs her name, and moves on.

Gracious—it is the one word that her friends, acquaintances, and staff use more often than any other to describe Lady Bird Johnson. Whether playing bridge with friends or attending a dinner with political associates, she puts an immediate halt to any conversation that verges on becoming gossip by quickly interjecting, with a firm note to her voice, "I only know she (or he) has always been kind to me." And the conversation ends. On a shopping trip, she will tell a saleswoman, "That dress just doesn't make my heart sing," rather than risk wounding the person's pride by saying, "I don't like that." On a walk around the LBJ Library grounds she will pause to encourage the gardener, asking both about his bad back and whether the azaleas have yet been mulched, or she will chat briefly with classes assembled on the grounds in spring. Her schedule is a busy one, but she manages to appear ever unrushed.

Lady Bird was born in Karnack, Texas, a small community near the Louisiana border that city fathers had intended to name after an Egyptian city but misspelled. "My daddy came just before the turn of the century, along with hundreds and hundreds of other young men to seek his fortune," she says. After Thomas Jefferson Taylor had established himself, he returned to Alabama and persuaded Minnie Lee Patillo to return as his bride. Claudia Alta Taylor was born when her two older brothers were eight and eleven years old, an age difference which many psychologists claim creates an "only child" environment for the youngest. Named "Lady Bird" by her family maid, she tried unsuccessfully for the next twenty years to be known as Claudia, but old friends kept her nickname alive. Years later, she laughed when she attended an international event, signing the guest register, after many Lady Janes and Lady Marys from around the world, with her own Lady Bird.

Her mother encouraged an early interest in literature and music, and through her urgings, a preschool program was started at the one-room schoolhouse for young Lady Bird to attend. But when Lady Bird Taylor was little more than five years old, her mother died following a fall and subsequent miscarriage. Her maiden aunt, Effie Patillo, moved to Karnack to help raise her.

"I think I was raised with more tenderness and, ah, gentle affection perhaps than my brothers were. They were away in boarding school and I was there, and Daddy was the kind to lavish his affection. I'm sure I had a most unusual sort of raising because Daddy was a very busy man, and Mother would have brought a sort of softening influence and social influence into his life. My aunt Effie sort of raised me, so to speak, and likewise, she encouraged me in many things, such as love of nature and interest in books and respect for the beautiful written word. But she was much too soft and gentle, and, well," Johnson says in a soft voice, then continues in a louder, frank statement of fact, "she was an invalid, so that she didn't exert a strong influence in discipline, no influence at all. I mean, normal mothers would have spent a lot of time trying to make sure that their children had companions of their own age who were 'nice' girls and boys," and she italicizes 'nice' so that the word conjurs up all maternal lectures from childhood on the broad subject of nice. "I grew up way out in the country and I hardly had anybody to play with," she recalls, adding, "but I didn't really miss it."

A quiet, dependable girl during childhood, with a reputation for thinking and acting responsibly, Lady Bird credits her family with fostering her belief in the value of independence. "My father was the most independent man I think I have ever seen and he had a great fear of being dependent. I think that, because he was so hurt by mother's loss at an early age, he felt 'Never again will I have that tie.' Then my aunt Effie was as totally and completely dependent as it is possible to be. She had many sweet, kind, loving virtues, but she was not well, not ever, and she depended first on her father, then my uncle Claude, then Lyndon and me to manage her business affairs for her. So I grew up having a great feeling of independence, both on the valuable side of having it, and on the painful, painful side of not having it."

After two years at a Dallas junior college for women, Lady Bird Taylor arrived in Austin to attend the University of Texas. As a student, she had her own car, an open checking account, and a charge account at Neiman-Marcus, privileges that set her apart from many but which her frugal nature forbade her to misuse. Although her first degree in 1933 was in education, she recognized that she did not want a career in the classroom, so she took a second degree the following year in journalism.

While she had never suffered personal deprivation, Lady Bird Johnson found no difficulty later in sharing Lyndon Johnson's dreams of a Great Society. "I never thought of having a political philosophy before I met Lyndon. I remember when I was at the University of Texas, and the Depression was on us, I personally didn't have to worry about it, because I just knew Daddy was going to take care of me. But I do remember hearing a tone in Daddy's voice I had never heard before when he called me up to say. 'Honey, the banks are closed. I hope that you wrote a check a few days ago so that you have some money. But I'm sending you the last dollar out of the cash register and I don't know when the banks will reopen.' I can't describe that as fear, but I knew he had come up against something bigger than he was, and that it sort of shook him. But I never felt that I was going to suffer from it."

She pauses, then continues in a quiet reminiscing tone. "Lyndon used to tell me that he would go into the cafe and look at what money he had, and that an egg sandwich was ten cents and the ham and egg was fifteen cents. He'd think about it real hard and he'd want that ham and egg, but he'd get that egg alone nearly every day, because he had to make his money last a certain length of time. And then every quarter, there came a time when you had to pay your tuition, which was the large sum of thirty dollars. He said that it was a traumatic experience, the week before tuition-paying time. He hardly ever had enough money to pay it, and so it was just 'maybe it will come and maybe it won't.'"

Recalling her first meeting with Lyndon Johnson, shortly after her college graduation, Lady Bird says, "I knew I had met something remarkable, but I didn't know quite what." The future president, at that time a congressional assistant to Representative Richard Kleberg, asked her to join him for breakfast the following morning at the Driskill Hotel. With some hesitation, for she recalled having a "sort of queer moth-in-the-flame feeling about the remarkable young man," Lady Bird Taylor met Lyndon Johnson, and following breakfast, they drove through the countryside around Austin. "He told me all sorts of things that I thought were extraordinarily direct for a first conversation—his salary as secretary to a congressman, about how much insurance he had, his ambitions, about all the members of his family. It was just as if he was ready to give me a picture of his life and of what he might be capable of doing." Then he asked her to marry him.

She answered neither affirmatively or negatively. But following constant pursuit from Lyndon Johnson and numerous conversations with trusted friends, she became Mrs. Lyndon Baines Johnson less than three months later in an Episcopal service in San Antonio. The nervous bridegroom forgot the wedding ring, and the ceremony was held up long enough for a friend to race to a nearby Sears and Roebuck store for a $2.50 ring.

The couple moved immediately to a small apartment in Washington, where Lady Bird Johnson managed the congressional assistant's monthly salary of $267 frugally enough to set aside $18.75 each month for a savings bond. When her husband became state administrator for the National Youth Administration, they returned to Texas. Within two years, when the congressman representing Texas' tenth congressional district died, Lyndon Johnson saw an opportunity to try for elective office.

"I had plenty of reservations, plenty of reservations, although not from the wisdom of knowing how hard a life it really is. But Daddy had not really thought much of politicians," she laughs. "At the university I had learned to think more of the worth and the hopes of our government and its administrators. But I really just didn't want him to run. The reason I finally went along and supported his decision was because he wanted to so VERY much. He had a great and wise friend named Alvin Wirtz, an excellent lawyer, a marvelous man who was a state senator for many years. I took a long walk with him and I asked, 'Senator, what do you think about Lyndon's chances?' And he said, 'I cannot tell you they are good.' He predicted a big field and said, 'It's most likely that Lyndon will be the least known, from the smallest county. But I do think that he will work harder, make more impression on those people he does meet, and I think he's got a great future. Just when, I don't know. I think, however, that his chances are as good now as they will ever be.' So I just decided, if Lyndon wants this, we better make the best.'' That first campaign was financed in largest part by $10,000 which Lady Bird Johnson borrowed against her inheritance from her mother's estate.

From that first campaign in 1937 until they left the White House in January 1969, Lady Bird Johnson proved to be an effective campaign force, a judicious sounding board for policy ideas, a constant link with the folks back home in Texas and, later, across the country. She was so shy about public speaking as a high-school senior that she was genuinely happy when she placed third in her class and was relieved of the task of giving a valedictory address. But, as a young congressman's wife Lady Bird realized that ''like it or not, I was going to have to stand up a number of times and at least say, 'Thank you for inviting me to this wonderful barbeque,''' so she enrolled in speech lessons in Washington.

When Lyndon Johnson, already in the naval reserve, asked for active duty during World War II, Lady Bird Johnson rented out their house, shared an apartment with long-time friend Nellie Connally, whose husband John also was serving in the Navy, and took over the task of running her husband's congressional office. She later credited that job with giving her the knowledge that, should it ever become necessary, she could make her own living. When President Roosevelt called back all congressmen serving in the armed forces to Washington in August 1942, Lady Bird Johnson found she missed the stimulus of working and was reluctant to return to the hostessing, tourguiding and the social afternoons expected of a congressional wife. She also wanted to establish a business of their own, in the event that her husband chose to leave public service.

She had hoped to purchase a Texas newspaper, but the one she wanted was too expensive. Instead, with a portion of her estate, she purchased KTBC, a small Austin radio station, which at that time was in the red. Lady Bird Johnson moved to Austin for six months and combed the ledgers, talked with personnel, studied operations and contracts, scrubbed walls in the building, all in an effort to turn the company around financially. Although she had never been faced with business problems, she was in part prepared by her Uncle Claude who, from the time she was a child, had sent her books on financial matters in preparation for the day when she would inherit the assets he planned to leave her.

When she finally returned to Washington, her station was showing its first small profit. KTBC was the nucleus of broadcasting holdings that eventually included television stations in Austin, Waco, Bryan, and Weslaco, Texas, and in Ardmore, Oklahoma. While

Johnson critics have charged that political influence helped advance the company's fortunes, few deny that Lady Bird Johnson's shrewd business acumen was largely responsible for the growth of the LBJ Company.

"My husband, from the time we were married when I was twenty-one, used to often remark about me that I had good judgment. And he'd say it with such pride that I would feel like I must try to HAVE good judgment," she laughs. "You know, there is such a thing as helping a person to be either prettier, or wiser, or more desirous of learning by just simply telling them that they are. I know, in the case of business, I felt that the main thing that I could try to achieve, do for it, was to evaluate people and choose good people and get them there, and make them want to stay by establishing a profit-sharing plan and by creating living conditions and working conditions that would mean as much continuity as you could have in that business."

Since Lady Bird Johnson moved from the White House back to the 438-acre LBJ ranch on the banks of the Pedernales in Stonewall, the requests for speaking engagements, political endorsements and public appearances have continued to pour in, keeping a full contingent of secretaries busy outside her eighth-floor office at the LBJ Library. She loves travel, whether taking her grandchildren to what has become an annual retreat to St. Johns Island, or touring Greece with friends, or travelling across the nation to encourage beautification. She was a very visible First Lady, and while she does not now seek the spotlight, neither does she shun it.

Her appearance has changed little since the days when she appeared regularly before the network lights, promoting her goal of national beautification. Her voice is soft, definitely Southern-slow. "No matter how it sounds, it always comes out in print as a drawl," she says, emphasizing 'drawl' until it seems a multisyllabic word. "Is it a drawl? I don't know." It is necessary to hear, rather than read, her words to totally comprehend her thoughts, for her speech is a pattern of italicized adjectives, uppercase exclamations, whispered emphasis.

Very few words come from her, however, that have not been thought out, judged before uttered. She is not a rash woman. Fellow board members at Texas Commerce Bancshares, Inc., where she is a director, say that she speaks rarely during board meetings but is listened to when she does, because she usually interjects both relevant and enlightening additions to the discussion. She is gracious during interviews, but even when discussing the suspense novels (she calls them "trash") that she reads for relaxation, Lady Bird Johnson is conversing carefully, not casually chatting.

Just when she thought she was finished with family campaigns, Charles Robb, husband of the older Johnson daughter, decided to run for Lieutenant Governor of Virginia, and Lady Bird Johnson helped stump that state for him. She had no words of advice for her daughter and son-in-law: "They really didn't ask me for any!" she admits with a chuckle. "Actually, Lynda Bird never dreamed that he would go into politics and didn't want him to, and was mad as hops that he did. But in the end, she loved him so much that she decided that she better put her all into it, which she did and did well." It was a lesson well learned from her mother.

Lady Bird Johnson says that her husband gave her most of the credit for rearing their daughters, but says, "That's not quite deserved, because they just both wanted to please him, and then, they knew how, if he ever got around to observing it, how hurt, angry, disappointed, and how . . . *articulate* he could be, if he found out they had done something that he thought was wrong. But I can't say that either one of us gets much credit for discipline. We simply sort of let them know what we thought they ought to do, we trusted them a lot, we gave them a lot of rein, and mostly they were real good, just real good, about living up to it."

Johnson says that if she were giving advice to young people today, it would be to watch their health, take good care of their bodies and "do something out of character once in a while. Don't seek the quiet eddy all the time. A little stress and adventure is good for you, if nothing else, just to prove you're alive," she laughs.

Although her family roots are in Alabama, and Lady Bird Johnson has affectionate sentiments for that state, she says that while growing up, "We had a STRONG sense of Texas, and of belonging to it and being proud of it, thinking it is special. I think it's been typical of the state of Texas, men, women and children, that we have always a lot of optimism here. There's a belief in ourselves and the world and the world's future. We just don't think it's going to come to an end, and we want to be an active part of shaping it."

Barbara Jordan

The non-stop flight from New York to Houston landed only minutes behind schedule, and the passengers, weary and stiff from the near three-hour flight, rose and began to disembark. One of those passengers, hampered by a noticeable limp, moved slowly from the plane and down the long passageway. Then, just before turning the corner into the terminal, she paused, took a deep breath, pulled herself ramrod straight and walked without a limp around the corner, to nod cooly and without encouragement to waiting reporters.

That determination, that inner strength, has come to be expected of Barbara Jordan. Since she gained statewide, then national, attention—first as a state senator and later as a congresswoman—she has come to represent uncompromising rectitude, moral authority, judicious reasoning and strength. In 1976, only four years after she arrived in Congress, a *U. S. News & World Report* survey of American leaders ranked her as the nation's most prominent woman leader. She had been mentioned as a vice-presidential candidate, United Nations ambassador, U. S. attorney general. The reporters awaiting her arrival in Houston that day wanted to know why—when she was not faced with advancing age, insurmountable scandal or terminal disease—why Barbara Jordan was not seeking re-election after serving three terms in the U.S. House of Representatives.

There was varied speculation over her decision. Some believed that her drastic weight loss of nearly one hundred pounds, reducing a frame once described as ''burly'' and ''massive'' to one more accurately labeled stately, and her limp, which she said was simply the result of an old knee injury, were signs of some serious disease. Jordan flatly denied those suggestions. Friends conjectured that she was, as one put it, ''Tired of suffering fools. In politics you have to suffer a lot of fools, and Barbara Jordan ran out of patience with that.'' With less elaboration than she used to describe her selection as ''Girl of the Year'' in high school, Jordan explained in her autobiography, *Barbara Jordan: A Self Portrait*, that she felt a responsibility to the country as a whole to speak out and define national interests. Remaining in Congress where time had to be spent ''doing things you really had no interest in doing'' only stood in the way of those goals.

One of her earliest goals, established firmly in childhood, was not to be ordinary, not to be, as she has often repeated, ''run of the mill.'' Born in 1936, the youngest of three daughters, in Houston's Fifth Ward, Barbara Charline Jordan was encouraged, even expected, to excel. Her father, a Baptist minister who earned his living working at a warehouse, had attended Tuskegee Institute; her mother, the daughter of a Baptist minister, had been an outstanding orator as a young woman. Years later, Barbara Jordan would remind interviewers that her father had scolded her for receiving anything less than excellent grades. As a student at Phillis Wheatley High School, Jordan competed successfully in national oratorical contests. After one successful contest when she was sixteen, Jordan commented on her victory to the Houston *Informer,* ''It's just another milestone I have passed; it's just the beginning.''

At Texas Southern University she distinguished herself as a debater and a speaker. She was the only woman on the debate team that defeated such opponents as Harvard University and Northwestern University. She graduated magna cum laude in 1956 and entered Boston University Law School. After receiving her LL.B. in 1959, she returned to Houston and, armed with a telephone and crisp, new business cards, set up her law office at the family dining room table. During the summer of 1960, she taught political science at Tuskegee Institute, the school her father had left because of financial problems in his senior year.

Within two years, Jordan opened a law office over a drug store on Lyons Avenue, but law was not her only interest. ''The extremes of opulent wealth and grinding poverty in Texas influenced me to try to do something to make things better for the disadvantaged,'' she says now, and that desire led her, by 1960, to take an active interest in politics. Again, her talent behind the speaker's platform moved her along quickly. When a speaker at a black church failed to show up for a speech in 1960, Jordan extemporaneously filled in. The response to her speech was so great that she was immediately relieved of envelope-stuffing duties and put on the speaking circuit for the Harris County Democrats.

In 1962, and again in 1964, she ran unsuccessfully for the Texas House of Representatives. Then in 1966, Houston electoral districts were redrawn as the result of a Supreme Court ruling. With no incumbent to face, Jordan was elected to the Texas Senate from a district in which thirty-eight percent of her constituents were black. She became the first black since 1883 and the first black woman ever to serve in the Texas Senate. In 1968, she was re-elected to a full, four-year term.

As a state senator, Jordan sponsored the establishment of a Texas Fair Employment Practices Committee, the creation of the state's first minimum wage law and the first increase in workman's compensation benefits in twelve years. She was voted the outstanding freshman legislator by her colleagues and was the first freshman senator ever appointed to the Texas Legislative Council, the research branch of the legislature. She was elected President pro tempore in March 1972, and when named governor for a day on June 10 of that year, she became the first black woman in American history to preside over a state legislative body.

As a member of the Texas Senate, Barbara Jordan developed a legislative style that later would serve her well in the U. S. Congress. Like a good student in the classroom, she had an edge over others because she always came to class, and she came prepared. She brought with her both a respect for the institutions of government and a willingness to work with the established powers already there. She once described herself as ''chipping away'' at the goals she had. Her willingness to work patiently and to compromise for partial victories, rather than take an unyielding stance, brought her equal amounts of praise and criticism throughout her political career. Although her votes generally reflected a liberal, democratic philosophy, she always managed to give the appearance of being independent.

The sheer power of her rhetoric often caused otherwise inattentive legislators to sit up and listen. Her voice is that of a seasoned actress, an impassioned missionary, a righteous headmistress, a lecturing parent. It can sound arrogant, soothing, indignant, supportive, reproving or understanding, depending on her intent. She is a diva who provides her own chorus, often repeating key words and phrases with a rhythmic cadence that gives her speeches an evangelical quality.

In the fall of 1972, Jordan won election to Congress from Texas' Eighteenth District, the first black woman elected from the South and the first woman from Texas to serve in Congress. With support from former President Johnson, she was appointed to the House Judiciary Committee, a position which catapulted her to national attention during the hearings considering impeachment of President Nixon in 1974. When she sat before the cameras and intoned, in her majestic cadence, the "We the People" speech and leveled a scholarly discourse on the constitutional and historical precedents for presidential impeachment, Jordan seized the nation's eyes.

Two years later she stood behind the podium at the Democratic National Convention in New York City. From the moment she pointed out that ". . . there is something different about tonight. There is something special about tonight . . . . I, Barbara Jordan, am a keynote speaker," until she ended her speech with Lincoln's words "As I could not be a slave, so I would not be a master," the ordinarily inattentive crowd gave her its rapt, applause-punctuated attention.

Although she pointed out frequently during her public career that she did not want to be a symbol—she repeatedly said "I'm not a professional black or a professional woman, but a professional legislator"—those two speeches stood as symbols of how far both women and blacks had come in the years since Barbara Jordan's first segregated oratorical competitions.

The most significant piece of legislation that Jordan sponsored as a congresswoman was the bill to extend and expand the Voting Rights Act of 1965, bringing Texas under its jurisdiction, over the protests of many state officials who claimed that the state was already working to eliminate voting discrimination because of language barriers. She was also the principal sponsor of a bill designed to guarantee consumers fair and competitive pricing by repealing federal authorization for state "fair trade" laws. She introduced a bill to provide Social Security benefits to homemakers, but it failed to gather enough support to pass.

After deciding not to seek re-election or another government position, Barbara Jordan accepted a professorship at the University of Texas Lyndon B. Johnson School of Public Affairs. The $38,000 position, established for persons who have had a distinguished career in public affairs, puts Jordan in the classroom, teaching intergovernmental relations and ethics to second-year graduate students. Spaces in her class are so coveted that a lottery system was devised to select students, who more or less win the opportunity to hear Barbara Jordan lecture, question and ponder the affairs of state.

"The greatest challenge as a professor is to be prepared for the students; to challenge them to give their best effort; and to stimulate them to think critically and analytically about public affairs problems," she says now. Friends say she is thrilled with her teaching job; she has frequently described herself as "walking on the ceiling" after a stimulating class session. When asked under what conditions she might again run for public office or accept a government appointment she responds, ''My career preference is the LBJ School of Public Affairs at the University of Texas at Austin.'' Although frequently mentioned as a possible candidate for the U.S. Supreme Court, Jordan has said she would not accept a seat on the Court if it were offered to her now.

Over-exposure in the press has destroyed more than a few public careers, but Barbara Jordan had a Hollywood press agent's shrewd sense of timing from the beginning of her ascent in the public eye. The more requests for interviews she receives, the fewer she seems to grant. Requests to ''sit in'' on her classes are granted only rarely. Except for small dinner parties for each of her UT classes, she restricts her entertaining to a few close friends, with dinner, guitar playing and singing at her home south of Austin.

For someone so long in the public eye, Barbara Jordan remains a rather mysterious, private person. If she has any long-range plans for the remainder of her life, she is a taciturn quarterback who keeps her plans to herself. During her adult years, she has given no more than six years at a time to any one venture: practicing law from 1960 to 1966, serving in the state senate from 1966 until 1972, Congress from 1972 until 1978. She once remarked that the Supreme Court was a place to retire to, and with her sense of timing, she probably would only accept that position, if tendered, when she plans to work only six more years.

Ninfa Laurenzo

When Ninfa Laurenzo decided in the spring of 1973 to open a small restaurant, a place where people could "get the kind of food Mexican people eat in their own homes," her son Jack laughed. After all, his mother had spent more time cooking lasagna than preparing enchiladas. But she had five children to educate, and profits from the small family busines were not sufficient. With $13,000 raised from mortgaging a second home on Houston's busy Navigation Street near the ship channel, Laurenzo turned a small house into a tiny restaurant with ten tables and seating for forty. She cooked; son Tommy washed dishes; other relatives waited tables.

When the doors closed July 3, after the first day of business, she and her five children were thrilled: gross profits for the day were $188. The brightly colored parrot trademark and "Gracias!" logo rapidly became as effective as Pavlovian bells in attracting customers. Little more than six years later, the number of restaurants had grown to six with four more scheduled to open, a catering business had flourished, and gross profits were well in excess of $10 million.

"Texas offers so much opportunity to people. And Houston is so dynamic. You can sell anything here, even shoelaces, if you work hard . . . and if they are good shoelaces," she says.

"I just knew we were going to make it, and when we began, there was no time left over to worry about failing. And everyday, more and more people came. We would be shocked by the lines waiting to come inside. We had a big celebration, the kids and I, the first time we broke a record by selling $1,000 on a Saturday. I mean, to us, that was just an unbelievable thing,'' Ninfa says. She is a jovial woman who greets all customers with a broad smile and often gives hugs to, or gets them from, the regular customers.

Ninfa Laurenzo is now Chairman of the Board of Ninfa's and every business day is a family reunion. Her oldest son, Roland, a graduate of the U. S. Naval Academy, is president of the company. Son Jack, a graduate of Boston College who undertook additional studies at M.I.T. and Harvard, is purchasing agent. Daughter Phyllis, a graduate of St. Thomas and the University of Houston's Conrad Hilton School of Hotel and Restaurant Management, is director of catering. Son Thomas, a student at the Conrad Hilton School, manages the Westheimer restaurant in Houston, and the youngest child, Gino, works whenever he is needed when he is not attending high-school classes. A battalion of Laurenzo's nieces, nephews, brothers, sisters, cousins and an assortment of in-laws fill positions in accounting, operations, diet supervision, floor managing, cooking and clerical jobs.

Restaurants weren't the first venture into the food business for Laurenzo. She met her future husband, Dino Laurenzo, in 1944 while visiting her twin sister in Providence, Rhode Island, and married him a year later. ''We were going to live there but I was hating the cold. It was just too much for me, and one day, after I fainted in the street, Dino said he had read in *U. S. News and World Report* that Houston was the fastest growing city in the country. So we moved here in May of 1948 and opened up our little food manufacturing business that summer. It was Rio Grande Food Products, and we made tortillas and other Mexican food products and Gino's Pizza. It was a mixture of my Mexican with his Italian culture from the start. My husband always said we made a beautiful combination.''

Ninfa Laurenzo and her husband worked together until his death in 1969. ''I always worked and when the children were old enough, they helped too. It was a beautiful life. So many families are separated so much of the time by the fact that everybody goes his own way to his own job. We were very fortunate to be able to work together. And after my husband died, I was prepared. I had been in business with him so therefore I had the background to continue. It was difficult at first, but then I wasn't paralyzed. So many women depend so much on their husbands and never really go out into the business world as we did together.''

While Laurenzo enjoys the luxuries that accompany financial success, she is just as enthusiastic about seeing her dream of a taco stand grow into a network of successful restaurants. ''I love the restaurant business. It's a people world, I've always loved people, and you meet so many in this work . . . . I count my blessings every day, because what else could I ask the good Lord for? I was able to keep my children together, out of trouble. They're in love with their business and they are able to take care of a business that helps so many, many other people. When you're speaking of over six hundred employees, plus their families, you're helping an awful lot of people. And that in itself is a great thing," Ninfa says.

All of the company employees, from management to waiters, participate in the company profit-sharing program. She has organized training classes in all phases of restaurant employment for new employees and for those who want greater responsibilities in the organization. "I think that you have to make people feel that they are part of its success. As long as there are people like this, and you are willing to share with people what the Lord has given you, then the sky is the limit on what you can do."

Laurenzo began turning down offers to sell her company not long after she served her first tacos al carbon. Although planning to expand the market for the specialities, she hopes to maintain a family-run business. "You can lose your identity if you sell out, and if the mother company wants you to low grade the food, you may have to. And we don't want that to happen," she says emphatically. That leads to talk of shopping woes, and she can talk tomato prices like a produce specialist. "I don't know why, but people always think that Mexican food has to be cheap. It's not. We use green peppers, real cream, real orange juice, and over six hundred crates of avocados a week. We pay almost ten times more for green tomatoes than when I started. I went to Spain last year and bought three kilos of saffron. I paid $1,500 a kilo! I tell the managers, 'Make sure we use the right amounts, but don't let anyone waste it.' That's a lot of money," she exclaims, grinning as she finishes her tirade against inflation.

With the purchase of one of the two Karem's restaurants in San Antonio, Ninfa began to move her marketplace beyond Houston. Within three weeks after the purchase was completed in 1979, Ninfa opened the doors to her new restaurant with a grand opening party for nearly two thousand guests. By the end of 1980, she expects to have opened a restaurant in Dallas, another in Houston, and to have selected sites for more. Already the menu has been altered so that the tacos al carbon, which helped make her famous but which soon appeared on bright signs outside competitor's buildings, have been renamed and trademarked as "Tacos a la Ninfa." Even the margarita has been renamed—becoming a "Ninfarita."

Laurenzo is up by six A.M. and at her office soon after. She goes through the mail, takes phone calls, attends executive meetings, arranges training sessions, and then makes it a point to visit one or two of her restaurants. Her business day usually is scheduled to end by seven in the evening, but people who are entertaining at one of the restaurants frequently will make a special request that Ninfa stay and eat with the party. "I have such a difficult time with my weight. It's always a constant problem, trying to eat only once a day and then trying not to seem ungrateful when people say 'sit down and eat with us' or 'join us for a drink.'"

Each restaurant has its "regulars," people who enjoy being recognized by the management. Whenever possible, the regulars are seated at tables they call "mine." And, whether she is at the smaller restaurant on Navigation or the enormous Gulf Freeway restaurant which seats over one thousand, Laurenzo recognizes her repeat customers—no easy feat in a business that feeds an average of six thousand people a day.

With her success has come great visibility in the Houston Hispanic community, as well as in the community at large. She was the first woman appointed to the seven member Houston Mass Transit Authority Board, and she knows pressure from that assignment may mount. "I think people are very anxious about mass transit, but they've got to give this thing an opportunity. Really, we should have started with mass transit at least ten years ago. It will take a couple of years before you see a tremendous amount of change; it will be unbelievable. We have to make it attractive enough to encourage the public to take it." Her appointment to the Board in 1978 was for two years, and she was reappointed when that term expired. "I think it's a great challenge. I am enjoying it," she says.

Laurenzo believes increased opportunities will be opening for Hispanics to work in local government. "I think we have to unite and be strong and we cannot fight each other . . . . We have to show people that we can do a good job, that we are capable of going in there and doing it. I had $16 in my pocket the day I opened this restaurant, and here I'm running a multimillion-dollar organization. It can be done. I was telling some of my colleagues the other day that city hall has been very, very poor about taking care of Hispanics, regardless of their ability to perform. Because you can count on one hand the amount of Hispanic people they have in top jobs. People want to do something, do something big. You want to feel that you're able to get to the top like everybody else. I mean, there is no sense in all these people running out and getting their education and not being able to apply it. It's just very sad. You've got to be given the opportunity. And the opportunity I think will come and will be here . . . . And we've got to apply ourselves."

Ninfa Laurenzo has been ''applying'' herself to her work for quite awhile. She was born in Harlingen, the youngest of twelve children. Her father, Esteban Rodriguez, a plumbing contractor in the Rio Grande Valley, had come to Texas in 1910 as a political exile from Monterrey. ''I was the baby, but I had to learn to cook. We all had to do our share. And my sister's husband had a chain of small groceries. When they would go off in the summer, I would manage the grocery stores for them. Mr. S. G. Garcia was a very, very strong influence in my life. He made me feel that at fifteen, I could manage a business. I think that is where the desire was born to be in business myself. And my husband was a great influence. He walked with God. He was such a great inspiration to us and he believed in me.

''And I think that some people are born with that innate feeling of 'I've got to do it ' and 'I can do it.' And I've always felt that I can do anything that I undertake. I decided to do it. Many people are defeatists, negative on everything. They are defeated before they try.

''I had a light heart attack in 1967, and then I felt like I was re-born, because I had a lot of time to think in the hospital. If we sit down and count our blessings, we're in great shape, all of us. I feel that as long as you live with that philosophy you can be happy, and you can do things. My ambition now is to have Ninfa's all over the nation. It's going to take a lot of good brains, a lot of people, a lot of work, but it can be done and we're going to do it.''

Carole Keeton McClellan

If you saw Carole Keeton McClellan waiting in her Ford station wagon in the junior-high carpool line, you might pick her out as a former president of the Austin Women's Tennis Association, or a girls' P.E. coach, both of which she once was. But you probably wouldn't pick her out as the mayor of Austin, which she became in 1977.

With a scattering of freckles across her face, an athletic build and quick movements, short blonde hair and pep-rally enthusiasm in her voice, McClellan doesn't look like a typical politician, and she didn't become one in an orthodox manner. Married during her senior year at the University of Texas, she taught government and women's tennis while her former husband was in law school. She had four sons (two are twins) in five years, took an active part in the Austin Junior League, which she served as president, and participated in United Fund city youth programs and efforts to support the local symphony orchestra.

"But then I decided that I could do without the teas and sandwiches with the crust cut off . . . and get involved instead in the issues of the day. I was tired of spending a lot of volunteer hours in nondecision-making positions. Having been a teacher and having kids, I got very interested in the school scene . . . . I had the feeling that most of those on the school board who were making the decisions were certainly concerned about the tax dollar, which is important. But I didn't think they were that concerned or really knowledgeable about what was going on in the classrooms . . . . I thought my experience kind of folded in perfectly with that time in my life. That's why I ran for the school board in 1972.'' She was elected a member for two years, vice-president for two more, and then became the first woman president of the school board in 1976. With a year left in her term, she decided to run for mayor.

"I decided to run for mayor because I've always had the feeling that I really like to be where the action is. At the time I ran for the school board, friends were saying, 'Why now! There's court ordered desegregation. It is the worst of times!' I liked to get into that, and in fact, the school scene had become slightly dull when I began to think about running for mayor. It was calm and working well, and the city scene had a lot of really important things happening. The city was about to get out of Brackenridge Hospital, the municipally owned hospital, which I felt the city ought to keep since it is the only trauma center in ten counties. Energy was an issue. I decided that the city scene looked really exciting, with the health, environmental and energy issues.''

Running in 1977 against nine male candidates, McClellan was the first woman to seek the mayoral post in Austin. She eventually won the election in a run-off that put her into office with 50.85 percent of the vote, the narrowest margin ever to elect an Austin mayor.

"Gender was definitely an issue in that first race," McClellan says. "Two days away from my run-off election, my opponent's press people called a press conference. They had the owner of Cisco's Bakery, a place where the male politicians usually hang around and have eats and drinks and talk about the political world, and Joe Manor, the owner of Hyltin-Manor Funeral Home. Their whole message was that Mrs. McClellan is a nice lady, but this job is just too tough for a woman. The funny part is that within hours of the newspaper headlines, I had a delegation of women at my campaign headquarters with T-shirts printed that said 'Women Eat at Cisco's' and 'Be Buried at Hyltin-Manor.' I think the T-shirts got us through that last twenty-four hours . . . .

"But really, after I was in office about six months, it didn't seem to matter to anyone that I was a woman. Nobody felt awkward about it.'' About her second mayoral campaign, McClellan says, "I was attacked or criticized or praised on the issues, but I don't think the fact that I'm a woman is on anybody's mind anymore.''

McClellan had anticipated a close race when she ran for re-election in the spring of 1979. She had just endorsed continuing Austin's participation in the South Texas Nuclear Power project, within days of the Three Mile Island nuclear accident in Pennsylvania and while *China Syndrome* was showing to packed theaters. She felt that her support of the project would cost her votes but says she felt a leadership responsibility. "That's why I stuck my neck out. I don't think it would have passed if I hadn't, but that's the kind of price you pay. Boy, there is no buffering on the local scene. You have immediate impact and it's a tough place to survive.'' Yet when the polls closed, she carried every precinct and won with more than seventy-seven percent of the vote, the greatest margin ever given an Austin mayor.

Her separation and divorce before the 1979 election never became a campaign issue. ''I think the county, and certainly Austin, is past looking at personal issues now. There are too many real issues that concern voters. My divorce had absolutely nothing to do with my political life, and I have never commented on it because of that fact. What I did do was hit it right up front and center. I was not going to leave anything to speculation and because of four young sons, I wanted to handle it right. So every step of the way, instead of reporters asking me, I just issued a press release, very short and to the point . . . . For my family's sake, I said I'd have no further discussion. Period. The newspapers immediately carried a two sentence thing and that was it.''

Her daily agenda reads like a combination of pages from *Business Week* and *Parents Magazine.* She attends meetings with bond analysts in New York, a once uncomfortable chore that she now looks forward to eagerly. ''We're triple A on general obligations and we were double A on Standard and Poor's but they just kicked that up to Double A plus. I think we'll go back up to triple A because we've done everything we can do to improve the financial condition, and they're just waiting to watch us a while.''

She attempts to schedule meetings and assign tasks to her aides during the morning, so she will be free to pick up her youngest son at school at two-thirty. Often he returns to the office with her, and while she returns calls and continues working, he entertains himself with soldiers, games and other toys stored in the sideboard behind her desk. McClellan tries to leave the dinner hour free, so she can cook the meal and help with homework. At night, after the children are in bed, she turns her attention to the folder of work she has brought home and does the family laundry around 2 A.M. when ''it's a good time for me and it is not during peak energy use,'' a personal reaction to the energy crisis that she feels will intensify quickly. A long night's sleep for the mayor is five hours.

''I decided a long time ago that my kids could benefit as much from the issues that I was involved with as they could if I were sitting in the confines of my home holding them on my lap all day long. We've literally gone from diapers to shaving while in public office. They're really good kids, and I'm proud of them. I take them with me, and I sometimes xerox a copy of what I do and take it home to them, particularly to the ones who are arguing a contrary point. With the South

Texas Project issue, two of my kids are for it and two are against it, and we have a healthy debate of issues right there at home.

"They all have their chores, and they understand that sometimes, like during the campaign, life will be unusual. They are going to be ready for the modern woman, because instead of saying 'Won't you stay home and bake a cake like mother used to do?' they'll go in and bake the cake. One of them specializes in folding clothes, another one really likes the clean-up detail."

McClellan was herself reared in a family where the issues of the day were debated around the dinner table at night. Her father, Page Keeton, was dean of the University of Texas Law School for twenty-five years and still teaches full-time in retirement. "I grew up in a household that integrated what was going on in the world with the family life, and I am a believer in that. My father sort of set the pace, encouraging my brother and me to directly address the problems and speak out. He always encouraged us to speak out, whatever our opinions were, if we had good reasons for doing it."

Childhood bedtime was different for McClellan and her brother Richard than it was for children raised on fairly tales. "My father would come in at bedtime. I was about four and Richard was three. He'd give us bedtime cases instead of bedtime stories. He'd lay out a lot of social problems and other facts in those cases, and he'd say 'You're the judge; what ought to happen?' He'd never tell us that we were wrong. He'd say, 'Well, maybe, in some remote country that might happen under different circumstances.' But then, he'd come in the side door and point it out, some other things you might think about."

McClellan ran for president of the class during her freshman year at UT. Her opponent's father, another UT professor, called Page Keeton advising him to tell his daughter that she should run as vice-president, that women were not supposed to run for the top position. Keeton kept the phone call to himself, until years later, making no mention of it after the UT campaign which his daughter lost. When she asked his advice about running for mayor, he said that it was her decision, but that he would support her in whatever she attempted. "That was always my father's attitude, and it still is. 'If you want to give it a try, I'll support you.' My mother has always been very supportive too. The political world was a new venture for her, but in the last campaign I got her out walking door to door, which is a whole shift from where she started," McClellan says.

McClellan credits many people with helping her win election, from a handful of friends who organized a sort of meals-on-wheels program for her family during the campaign, to Claire Korioth, an

Austin friend. "She ran my first campaign for the school board when I didn't even know what a card file was. Claire just did it singlehandedly out of my kitchen. She is the first person I called when I began to think seriously about running for mayor, to see if she could spring loose from her job to help me. And there are a lot of people behind the scenes, a lot of women and a lot of men too, who help women, who made campaigns possible in a supportive, quiet way. One of the people who helped me the most is Liz Carpenter. She is doing more, I think, to build up the old girl network versus the old boy network in this state. She is totally supportive. Whatever it is you've done, she is totally supportive of you as a woman being out there and doing something."

McClellan refuses to speculate over any future political plans. She intends to go to law school someday, but says she is too "childrened for that now . . . . I really enjoy the political world and I like what I'm into and I don't want to, by any means, imply that I'm ready to stop. I just don't want to say I'm going to be here two years and then two years from now I want to run for such and such. I love the political world and I like to be in the decision-making role. Though I don't have any game plan, neither have I shut any doors."

Gabrielle McDonald

Testimony in the courtroom had dwelled on one subject: if and when the defendant had had access to an important set of keys. Finally, it was time for the lunch recess. All stood as Gabrielle McDonald, U. S. District Court Judge, recessed the court and walked to the door to her private chambers. Repeated attempts to turn the door knob failed, and eventually, with desperation fringed with humor, she turned to the nearly empty courtroom and asked, "All right, who HAS the keys?" Like most closed doors she has encountered, this one was quickly opened.

Her reputation as an attorney for complainants in job discrimination cases was established by successful lawsuits against corporate Goliath's such as Southern Pacific, Phillip Morris, Armco Steel, Long Star Steel, and Schlumberger. But when Gabrielle McDonald learned in mid-1977 that she was being seriously considered for appointment to the federal bench in Texas' Southern District, she was surprised. Her friends and husband had encouraged her to submit her resume, but as a young, black, female attorney who had battled against job discrimination on behalf of others all day long, she did not dream that a federal judgeship was a realistic job opportunity for herself. When her appointment to the $54,500-a-year lifetime position was confirmed, she became the first black federal judge in Texas, only the third black woman to rise to the federal bench in the country, and at age thirty-six, one of the nation's youngest federal judges.

Once all those "first" categories have been duly noted, she would prefer that they be forgotten. "I got so tired, after I was nominated and sworn in, of reading 'first black woman' after my name. I just wanted to be recognized as Gabrielle McDonald, U. S. District Court Judge. Well, since I've been on the bench, whenever decisions are reported in the newspapers, there has never been a mention that I was even black. That surprises me,'' she says.

Her interaction with other federal judges, she says, is minimal. ''I don't know how much they socialize with each other because the judges here are very, very different. We have some Republicans and some Democrats; we have some judges in their sixties and some in their forties and then myself. All . . . are men except me, so I still feel a little bit out of it in that I don't feel like 'one of the boys,' because I'm not. I still have the same feeling I had as a lawyer, a difference in terms of rapport, even comparing how my husband would relate to lawyers in a particular case and how I would relate. We would relate differently because, you know, he would play tennis with the lawyers on the other side and that kind of thing and I don't do that. Maybe it's just because I'm a woman and maybe it's because I'm still more standoffish because of my eastern influence. But there is a difference and I'm not one of the boys. But, then, that may be true for some of the other judges as well.''

During an earlier meeting, months before, as she waited for Senate confirmation and prepared for her move to the federal courthouse, she took a break from her packing chores to talk. She spoke openly about her family influences, her own elementary-age children, who grin shyly from the gold frame on her desk, her years of battle against discrimination. She is more reticent when asked to talk of her success as an attorney.

''Sometimes I've wondered whether I've accomplished anything at all,'' she reflected. ''If a case is a class action, you get a lump sum of money and perhaps you get changes in the way jobs in that one company are allocated. And then tomorrow, there's another company, or at the same time you have a docket of fifty, sixty other cases involving the same issues. So it's a constant battle to have the same problems solved. I kind of feel that there is still too much of this kind of litigation around. There shouldn't be. I have friends on the other side who defend these cases and they tell me that this whole process of litigating class actions has made a significant change in employment practices. But there is such a big job to be done.''

She believes there is probably more sex discrimination than race discrimination in employment practices. ''I think it's more pervasive and more acceptable. I think it's also harder to deal with. In terms of litigation, you will still have cases where an employer will say 'This is not a woman's job.' Or, in the interview process, they'll say, 'Well, what does your husband say about your taking this position?' I think minority women themselves have self-defeating thoughts. That's only because, you know, you've been pushed down so long and put in a role so long, you kind of feel that's the way it's supposed to be.''

To eliminate sex discrimination in employment—not only legally but also in actual practice—will take, she says, ''just time I guess. The process of more women going into jobs and fields that have been traditionally filled by males will bring about change. I don't think there is anything that can be done other than for things to happen. I mean, you can talk about them; you can have groups and raps; you can talk all you want. But when a woman like me, for example, becomes a judge then I'm sure that another black woman thirty years old now wouldn't feel that the likelihood of her becoming a federal judge is so remote that she really doesn't believe that it's even worth pressing for.''

McDonald learned early in her life to believe in herself and her ability to accomplish goals; it is a belief that she credits her late mother, a writer and editor with Prentice-Hall, with developing. ''My mother and I were tremendously close. She didn't really push me; she encouraged me. My mother had the attitude that showed me that she really respected me and she really made me feel good about myself. She just assumed that I was going to do well, and to do less was not doing what I should be. When I goofed-off in the ninth and tenth grades and brought home D's in algebra and first-year Latin, she didn't punish me. She just said, 'This isn't anything at all like what you're capable of doing.' You sometimes latch onto other people's values, until you decide what you want to do in life and develop your own values. So I had hers. Inside myself, I felt I was capable of doing great things, because I knew she believed I was capable of doing great things.

''My mother was very bright, and she read a lot and talked to us about what she read. And she was so proud and so loving. I really hope to bring that to my own children, that affection and warmth. It's so important to love your kids—physical, hugging love—and she was that way.''

McDonald was born in St. Paul, Minnesota, and following her parents' divorce when she was five years old, she moved to East Harlem with her mother and younger brother. Her memories of school-day Harlem include ''coming out of school one day on a fire drill and seeing the chalk outline of a human being who had been shot the night before. You just marched right over it.'' She and her brother (now an attorney) spent a year in boarding school in Pennsylvania until her mother and step-father moved to Teaneck, New Jersey, where McDonald attended predominantly white schools until she graduated from high school there.

Her freshman year at Boston University, McDonald remembers, was "Just partying . . . . Then I transferred to Hunter College, and that's when I really decided I was going to buckle down. I became really intense about grades, as I was later in law school, and am now with my own children. Hunter was a free university at that time, but once you got in you really had to study very hard to stay there. We didn't have any money for me to go anywhere else, so I stayed and studied. The competition was very keen and that was the turning point for me."

McDonald entered Howard University to study black history but soon changed her mind and enrolled in the law school there. After graduating first in her law class, she went to work as an attorney for the NAACP and while employed by its Legal Defense and Educational Fund in New York, she met Mark McDonald, the Fund's local counsel at that time in Houston. They married in December 1968 and began private practice together in Houston.

Recalling her own childhood, when her mother worked, she says, "I used to race my brother home from school, start dinner, do my homework, watch *American Bandstand,* fight with my brother. It was quite a normal childhood." Her own two children are in a house-keeper's care after school until McDonald returns home from work in the evening. When her schedule as an attorney permitted, McDonald drove home during the day to see that a sick child got "soup and hugs" and took her turn at driving son Michael on school field trips. As a judge she is usually out of the courthouse by early evening in time to read stories to her daughter, Stacy, who playfully calls her mother "Judgie."

Combining the roles of wife, mother and professional is hard, she says, but not impossible. "All those things are potentially full-time jobs, and I think it's a question of realizing that you cannot be one hundred percent performing in each of those categories all the time. You just have to shift priorities at different times. And husbands should learn how. I think this is a problem with some men. I think husbands can play a great role too, because, if they are truly behind you in your career, they must shift priorities also." There is little doubt in Gabrielle McDonald's mind that she can shift those priorities, accomplish her jobs, and do them all well.

Although she arrived in Texas as a skeptical New Yorker, expecting cactus and cowboys in downtown Houston, she calls herself a Texan now and talks about the frontier spirit she believes can be found in the state. "I think people are different in Texas. I don't know how many of the people are from Texas and how many have come to Texas. But I do believe that people, once they are here, believe they can do things. They tend to have a greater belief that they can accomplish things. We're still, in a sense, the frontier. Things are kind of tight and locked in, in New York for example. But the attitude here is that you can move and you can grow and you can do more. The stereotypes about people being more friendly and more open are true, with both men and women. I will encourage my own children to spend time in the East, I will make certain they do, because I want to expose them to different people. But if I could pick a place for them to grow up and live forever, I would pick Texas.

"Don't misunderstand me. Don't let me tell you that I think I can do anything, or that women, particularly black women, can do anything. I think that we all recognize that there are very serious limitations on where we can go, and we're still living in a society, unfortunately, where judgments and decisions are made by other persons sometimes on the basis of race and sex. I'm not suggesting that it's all wide open. I'm saying that there is a feeling of wide open opportunity, and there is definitely a difference in terms of your potential for growth. I see a greater opportunity for individual growth."

As an attorney, McDonald could tally her successes in numbers of cases won, settlements awarded, employment practices altered. As a judge, success will be more difficult to evaluate. "I want to be sure that all litigants and all the attorneys have a fair trial. If I can convince people that I truly care about justice, because I do, and that I am truly impartial and fair and patient, and that I will listen and give lawyers courtesy, then I will be pleased with my reputation as a judge."

Dr. Alice McPherson

Even on Saturday afternoons, the waiting rooms at McPherson & Associates in Houston are filled. Families close ranks around the older patients; a mother sits reading to her young son as her husband listlessly stares at the unturned pages of *Time* magazine; other couples wait silently. They are referred patients, waiting to see Dr. Alice McPherson or one of her associates.

A giant in the specialized medical field of ophthalmology, McPherson stands little more than five feet tall. With bouffant blonde hair perfectly in place, deep dimples that punctuate a girlish laugh and sparkling, clear blue eyes, Dr. Alice McPherson, without her white physician's jacket, looks like a woman who would spend her day off getting a manicure and comb-out. Instead, she has examined and counseled a steady stream of patients, returned calls related to the Retina Resarch Foundation of Houston, which she heads as president and research director, and scheduled operations for the coming week.

When McPherson completed her specialized training at the Retina Service of Massachusetts Eye and Ear Infirmary in 1952, she was the only female retina specialist and surgeon in the world. She is the first female member of the Gonin Club, an international organization established for the elite in her speciality, and the only woman ever elected to serve as its president. She is also a past president of the Retina Society. There are now, perhaps, two or three other female retina surgeons in the country she says, and a few more about the world, but certainly not enough to plan a large convention soon.

Canadian-born McPherson ''became bound and determined'' at thirteen to pursue a career in medicine. She had already considered a social service career, but says, ''I saw that in the field of social work, I wouldn't be able to make any sweeping changes. In medicine, on a one-to-one basis, I would be able to help anyone, anywhere, despite language, religion, any of the things that separate people. I would be able to help the young, the old, a wide range of people.''

Hers was not a medical family, and her father discouraged his first-born from medicine, certain that she would tire of the long years of education or marry, raise children and not practice. To prove her determination and pay for her own education, McPherson worked summers during high school and college, holding two jobs at a time, and worked part-time during undergraduate years at the University of Wisconsin. When the time came for medical school, just as she was beginning to wonder if she could attend school and work at a job too, her father capitulated, recognized his daughter's determination and paid the bills.

As a young child, Alice McPherson believed that of all handicaps a person could suffer, the loss of sight would be the worst. This belief led her to ophthalmology. When she chose her speciality, one well-known ophthalmologist told her, ''Ophthalmology is a prestige field for men and the mathematical requirements will be too much for you.'' She recalls, ''I didn't say anything, but I thought to myself at the time, 'You don't know me, buster, but I made all A's in calculus and if I want a career in opthalmology, I will have it.'''

Despite the early bit of chauvinistic advice, McPherson says she has never felt discrimination because of her sex. She jokes about the appeal of her speciality, saying ''It's neat and tidy, and we women are so good at petit point and needlework!'' But she has believed, since her selection from a field of five hundred applicants for a class of seventy medical students, that merit is the major yardstick for measurement in her field. ''Opportunities in the early forties were perhaps not as great for women in business. But, unlike many professionals, you must stand on your own merits in the scientific field. All of the associates here are men, and we don't talk about a surgical procedure, saying, 'How would you as a male or a female surgeon handle this?' I guess you could say the profession is asexual,'' she says. As for the reaction of patients, McPherson says, ''I believe some patients prefer women doctors because they believe women are much more sympathetic. But I find the public doesn't really think about whether a doctor is male or female.''

After practicing briefly in the Boston area in the early 1950's, McPherson interviewed in several areas of the country and chose to establish her practice in Texas. She practiced three years at a clinic in Temple, Texas, then moved to Houston. "One of the things I liked was the clean air and lack of traffic," she laughs. "Of course that's changed now, but the factors which really made me choose Texas remain the same. There was and still is a friendly, welcoming population. In the medical community there was and remains an atmosphere of opportunity, a pioneer drive, a desire to lead, not just follow, medical research." In the tradition of Texas, she became one of those pioneers. "Houston received one of the first five ruby laser machines in the country, and one of the first couple of machines using liquid nitrogen for repairing retina damage. By choosing to come to Texas, I have had an opportunity to use some of the finest equipment in the world in the very earliest years of its development." McPherson joined the staff of Baylor College of Medicine in 1959 and continues to serve there as a clinical professor of ophthalmology and chief of the Retina Service.

McPherson enters the operating arena three days a week, beginning her surgical agenda at 7:30 in the morning and often not leaving before 7:30 at night. Each patient is advised that the operation may last from two to five hours. Three more days a week, she is in her office, often arriving before her staff and leaving long after them in the evening.

Many of the retinal problems McPherson encounters are the result of diabetes, and she says that diabetic retinopathy, a progressive vascular degeneration of the retina, soon will be the number one cause of blindness. "Because great strides have been made in treatment of diabetics, the people with this disease are living longer. They used to die before the eye problems, which came with increasing age, developed. They weren't living long enough to have children who were diabetic in turn. Now statistics show that one out of five of us are carriers of diabetes."

The other leading problem she sees is muscular degeneration, an aging of the eye related to the basic process of aging itself. "Can you prevent aging? Certainly good living patterns, good nutrition, good basic health seem to slow the process. People with hypertension or diabetes are more prone to eye problems. But sooner or later, if a person lives long enough, the eyes will show aging. I wish we had more to offer, but there are certain tissue changes that we just can't control. We do what we can, and we hope through research to be able to do more."

Her desire to discover the causes of and effective methods of treating diseases of the retina, as well as means of preventing those diseases, led McPherson to help set up the Retina Research Foundation in 1969. The Foundation, a non-profit organization that supports research in several institutions, was made possible by one of McPherson's patients, an attorney without heirs, who bequeathed his estate to further McPherson's research work. The Foundation also seeks public support through contributions from individuals, corporations and other foundations.

While long-range research continues through the Foundation, McPherson continues her day to day battle against retinal disease in the operating room. She compares what she does to a good welding job. Tears and holes in the sensitive, very thin retina can produce retinal detachment and blindness. By using a zenon arc, ruby laser or argon laser, McPherson creates tiny burns on the retina which act like tacks to hold the retina in place. Another method used is cryotherapy, or freezing. "We put a probe on the outside of the eyelid, and the freezing, using liquid nitrogen, takes place on the tissue but it only affects the most sensitive layer, the retina. It acts like a glue. Holes and rips can more or less be put together," she says.

Her work often creates great tension and emotional exhaustion for McPherson. "If all goes well, there is a feeling of elation. But other times, when you do all you can but the prognosis is not good for the patient, it is very depressing. Accidental injuries are only a fraction of my schedule. I don't have anything easy like fitting glasses or red eyes. And it is hard, day after day, to go from room to room to room, to problem after problem after problem. The other bad thing is that you can never spend enough time with people. You try to give and give of yourself, but no matter what you do, there is the feeling that you should have given more, spent more time in conversation, done more."

By the end of a day, when patients have been kept waiting because of an emergency and phone calls have stacked up, McPherson says the tension causes her to become "snappy" at the women who work in support positions for her. "I'm not really snapping at them; I'm letting off steam, because when I walk into that room with a patient, I'd better be calm and nice and solve his problems the very best that I can."

When she walks into a patient's room, an assistant claims, "The patient takes priority. It's like Dr. McPherson clicks a switch, and in her mind, that patient and his problems are the only things in the world. She can concentrate such total attention on each individual."

McPherson used to play golf for relaxation but found it too time consuming for her six-day-a-week schedule. Although she now enjoys an occasional swim in her pool at home, she mainly credits her husband with helping her to relax and forget the day's demands. "My

126

husband is wonderful . . . . so easy to get along with. He is a realtor and very easygoing. If I go home and get too irritable and get to snapping at him, he just turns up the radio or pretends he doesn't hear. Later on he may say something funny to make me laugh. He really is quite wonderful to me as a counterbalance.''

Because she wanted to establish her career first, McPherson married later than many women. ''I was so career oriented,'' she says, ''that I didn't want other responsibilities. My husband was a golf pro before we married, and he could travel to visit me wherever I was serving my internship or residency. That went on for ten years until we married. By then he appreciated how devoted I was to medicine.'' McPherson decided not to have children because, she says, ''I didn't know if I could do the children justice. Rearing children is a serious responsibility.''

The many books she has written and edited, the papers she has read at scientific gatherings, her position as an officer of the American Academy of Ophthalmology, her responsibilities as head of the Retina Fellowship program at Baylor, all her many endeavors combined with her surgical schedule make free time a rare thing for Alice McPherson. ''But you cannot call that a sacrifice,'' she exclaims, ''because these are options which I have chosen quite willingly.''

128

Nancy Brown Negley

Nancy Negley rushes into her San Antonio home, breathlessly apologetic because a museum meeting has detained her. Only an hour earlier she had accepted a large financial gift on behalf of the San Antonio Museum Association, and she was still ebullient, launching into a rapid-fire discussion about museum and conservation plans. Her involvement with the arts in Texas and on the national level has become a career, demanding her time, energy and imagination.

As vice-president of the American Archives of Art, a division of the Smithsonian Institution, Negley was instrumental in bringing five study centers to Texas cities. These centers, supplied with microfilm and readers, make permanent collections of the Smithsonian, the Metropolitan Museum of Art and other museums available for viewing by Texas art enthusiasts. "Portions of the collections of the great museums must be stored rather than exhibited. The microfilm study centers are the best way we have now of spreading the collection of magnificent works and knowledge out to the rest of the country, of decentralizing art."

Negley has been an executive officer or board member of many art related organizations: the San Antonio Conservation Society, the Texas Fine Arts Society, the San Antonio Museum Association, the Southwest Craft Center, the National Museum Services Board, the Archives of American Art and the National Trust for Historical Preservation. And she will argue vehemently with anybody who minimizes the effects of such volunteer work.

''For the individual, you can't buy the kind of experience you can get in volunteering services. You have a full spectrum of work: from scrubbing floors and mending pots at the museum and passing out bumper stickers during a campaign, to arranging schedules, raising money, determining policies at the board level. It is far more exciting than a single job and brings you in touch with a greater variety of responsibilities. People who do volunteer work have to be as much, or more, responsible than if they were in a paid job.''

Like many women who pursue volunteer careers, Negley is quick to point to the ''free labor'' and other economic benefits that volunteers give to their local communities and the state. ''Cities couldn't afford to pay for the thousands of free volunteer hours they get in different areas of charitable, cultural and civic work each year from Texas women. And beyond that, the cultural developments in a city can mean economic benefits to many citizens. King Tut should have taught us that the arts can bring so much to a city . . . . Unlike conventions, where it's all canned money going only to a small group of hotels or restaurants, when an exciting art exhibit comes into a city, large sums of money are spent throughout the city and it is far more lucrative to all of business.''

Negley agrees with the sign over the entrance to the Massachusetts art school she attended which advised ''Art IS Business.'' She was one of several board members of the San Antonio Museum of Art to convince the federal Economic Development Agency that growth of the arts was a sound business investment for the city's tourism industry. The agency made a $2.5 million grant to help fund the new San Antonio Museum of Art. The complex of red brick buildings in a lower socioeconomic portion of the city was once a brewery, then cotton mill and ice house, and is listed in the National Register for Historic Places. The project delights Negley because it combines both art and conservation with business.

Nancy Negley has the tweedy, scrubbed-face look and the boarding-school polish of one born to an aura of noblesse oblige. Her parents raised her to believe that service to the community was ''not only a responsibility but a tremendous privilege.'' Raised in Houston with a governess and formal family dinners, as the oldest child in a family of three daughters, Negley first earned her allowance by mowing lawns. Before many summers passed she realized that drawing and painting would be easier, and she began selling her own art work to her father, negotiating feverishly over prices. It was then that her interest in art began, she recalls.

Her father, Brown & Root Construction Company co-founder George Brown, was at the center of Lyndon Johnson's powerful circle of supporters. Because her mother "hated politics," Negley attended political dinners and rallies in her place. "I cannot remember not going. I was very young; it was before I entered my teens, and it was dazzling for a youngster. To this day I love politics." Smoke-filled rooms where political careers might start or end, dinners with long speeches and campaign trips across the state are among the fondest memories of her youth and later led her to serve as vice-chairman of the state Democratic party.

After graduating from St. Mary's Hall, a girls' preparatory school in San Antonio, Negley studied art for two years in Boston. Soon after she returned to Texas, she married and moved with her husband, Alfred Negley, to his ranch in western Texas. (They were divorced in 1978.) Her energies there were spent doctoring cattle, riding horses, cooking for the men and organizing study groups for women friends. When Negley's ranching interests expanded into marketing the cattle, the Negleys returned to San Antonio, and Nancy Negley immediately began participating in political and cultural organizations in the city.

"No one realizes how demanding political life is, how grueling it can be for the family. After a while, I decided I preferred a private life. When my three children were growing up, I realized at one point that I was giving more time to other people than I was to my family. It was more than I was willing to give then."

As her leadership role in politics decreased, her interest in promoting the arts and conservation increased. "With conservation and art, you can see your contribution. In politics, you work like crazy to get something done, and someone comes along and undoes it. In working for the arts and conservation in a community, you leave something for generations to come."

Although Nancy Negley now prefers engaging in low-key, behind-the-scene political activities and letting "new blood" take leadership positions, her interest in politics remains strong. She believes that the arts, conservation, politics and business are all interrelated. "Sooner or later, those of us interested in the arts, who love them for what they are and believe in what they contribute to the community, will have to lobby together to receive funds and the support necessary to continue . . . . Art serves a universal truth. Great paintings . . . bring enormous joy into our lives. Why not let a small fraction of the tax dollar give us this?"

And if that sounds political, "Well," she says, "politics means education, in the original sense of the word. Women who volunteer have to get into politics. You cannot be in any field where you are serving the public without getting into politics.

"And, my dear, there's politics in everything!"

Mary Moody Northen

When her father, William Lewis Moody, Jr., died in 1954, Mary Moody Northen, past retirement age herself, became president of more than fifty companies and corporations. Only months later, her husband also died. Although she had shared her father's interest in commerce since her childhood, she recalls, "I had never had an office, never worked a day in my life. Then overnight, I was faced with that responsibility. I didn't see how I was going to do it. Often I was downtown working until nine or ten at night. But I just did the best I could, and fortunately I met with success."

It is nearly impossible to discuss the history of Texas without discussing her family. Her great-grandfather on her mother's side, Charles Shearn, had come to Texas from Bath, England, with his wife and two children. "I can't believe he would do that with a family. Now, you could understand leaving England for the frontier if he had been a young, independent bachelor," Northen comments. As a child she often heard stories of Charles Shearn, of his capture and sentence to death by the Mexican army, only to be saved by his young son (and her grandfather) who ingeniously insisted in broken Spanish that they were not Texans but subjects of the British crown. Charles Shearn, as a Texan, later signed the first Texas Declaration of Independence at Goliad.

Northen's paternal grandfather, William L. Moody, Sr., moved from Virginia to Fairfield, Texas, in 1854, and later settled, with the rank of colonel, in Galveston at the close of the Civil War. Colonel Moody established a cotton factorage business, loaning money against future crops, and soon after added banking to his enterprises. His son, William Lewis Moody, Jr., joined the family business in 1886 and subsequently expanded the Moody interests to include ranching, newspapers, hotels, and insurance, creating one of the largest financial empires in the United States. When a Texas law of the early 1900's required all insurance companies active in the state to invest their funds in Texas, most companies abandoned Texas for states with less stringent laws. Moody, Jr., seized the opportunity to hire already trained but no longer employed insurance agents, and his American National Insurance Company grew rapidly to become one of the largest insurance companies in the Southwest.

For Mary Moody Northen, a drive through Galveston is a glance at a personal diary still being written. As the chauffeur drives her from her Victorian home to her contemporary office downtown, she sees both the historic homes, where as a sheltered young girl she attended teas and cotillions, and the new commercial construction, often financed by her family corporations.

As a young girl, the oldest child in a family of four children, Mary Moody's interest in business was encouraged. ''My father knew I was interested in what he did. We were very close and very much alike. So he would often talk to me about what he was working on, what decisions he made. Sometimes he would give me statements or proposals to look at. I'd wait until he went to bed at night, and then I'd study them, and we'd talk about them the next morning at breakfast. Sometimes I'd call his attention to things that I didn't think were just as they should be. And when I didn't understand something, he would explain patiently. And when I found errors or suggested changes he considered worthwhile, he was very proud.''

Northen was a frail child whose poor health kept her at home with tutors for much of her schooling. She recalls, ''All I wanted to do was sit in the house and read and study. One year the physician told my tutor he didn't want me to have to memorize anything because it would be bad for my health. So I spent the year reading and discussing literature. My tutor wanted to take me to the beach to study, but my mother wouldn't hear of it.''

Her parents' business and social interests kept them traveling often, and Mary Moody and her two brothers and sister usually traveled with them. ''I find most parents these days leave their children at home, but my parents never left us. We went to New York nearly every time my father was there on business, and then we'd go down to Virginia. We have roots rather deep in Virginia, so we always spent summer at Mountain Lake where it was always cool in the summer. Later on my father built a new hotel which is still there." Her interests in art, music and historic preservation were born and nurtured during these childhood visits to Virginia.

As her health slowly improved during childhood, her father urged her to share his love both of business and nature. One summer she was given several hens to raise. "My grandfather ordered me a subscription to a national poultry magazine. It came, addressed to 'Mary Elizabeth Moody, President, The Great American Chicken Company.' I did sell eggs to my mother for a while, but I petted all the chicks so much that most of them died," she laughs. Soon after her father presented her with a small pony, she was riding the ranch horses when the family traveled to one of the twelve Moody ranches throughout Texas, Oklahoma, and West Virginia. "Some parts of the country were quite rough and had steep paths. My friends would be afraid to go where we rode. When I had to take the lead, I had to ride almost backwards urging them to come on. I haven't ridden in a long time now, but I think I could," she says firmly.

A sheltered, shy young woman, Northen remembers that, when the time came for her debut in the thirty-room family home, she "knew only one young man in Galveston .... I didn't go out socializing like so many young girls. I only knew that young man because he worked for one of my father's interests and would come by to talk over business matters with my father."

When she was nineteen, she met Edwin Clyde Northen who had come to Galveston to study medicine. Soon after they met, he decided to enter business and established an insurance agency. They were married in 1915, and much of her time during their near four decades of marriage was spent encouraging developments in the arts in the Gulf Coast area. Preservation of historic buildings has long been at the top of her lengthy list of priorities, for she can vividly recall the great hurricane that struck Galveston in 1900, killing more than six thousand people and leaving few buildings undamaged.

"We were sitting out the rains in my parents' home, but one of the servants, a young German girl, went outside and tasted the water. She came back inside and said it was quite salty. Then we knew the Gulf and the bay were coming in and that it was not just another rainstorm. We finally went to my grandfather's three-story brick house. As the rains entered the first floor there, my mother took us upstairs while my father stayed on the first floor and assisted the people who sought refuge." As soon as travel was possible, the children and their mother left for Houston on the first boat to leave Galveston. "There were uprooted trees and debris in the bayou. My mother always said afterward that, as bad as the hurricane was, traveling to Houston was worse. It took us nearly a day to travel up Buffalo Bayou. There was no ship channel then," she says.

Returning to her ravaged hometown, eight-year old Mary Moody felt concern for the many damaged homes and buildings. This concern, fueled by her parents' belief in the value of a sense of history, later led her to devote thousands of hours to historic preservation projects, culminating in her selection as honorary chairman of the Galveston Historical Foundation. Her first personal philanthropic gift was toward restoration of Washington-on-the-Brazos, and many of the letters that fill her mailbox daily concern preservation efforts across the state.

"Often my own doorbell will ring, and when we answer it, people will ask when the next tour is. They think that my house is the Bishop's Palace or Ashton Villa," she laughs. Her home, which once belonged to her parents, has more than enough wall space should she decide to display her five honorary degrees, numerous certificates of service, and hundreds of awards from the many organizations to which she belongs. She is the only woman to serve on the Foundation Board of Virginia Military Institute, and the only honorary woman alumna of VMI. She is an associate of both Rice University and the University of Texas and is on the board of directors of Hollins College in Virginia. Although she never had a child of her own, Mary Moody Northen's support of the Boy Scouts of America has earned her local, regional and national awards, and she also is an honorary member and the sweetheart of a nearby local troop.

Her long-held dream of an outdoor amphitheater for Galveston was realized in 1978. After breaking ground for the 1,800-seat theater at the controls of a bulldozer, she was disappointed that she could not add the bulldozer to her collection of ground-breaking shovels. "I had attended an outdoor theater many years before with my husband, and we talked then of how much we wanted one for Galveston. This city has a long, eventful past, and I wanted a place where people could come and enjoy the historical story of Galveston and Texas in a setting that is part of a beautiful Galveston today."

Once the amphitheater in the new Galveston Island State Park began filling with crowds, she turned her attention to another project, the creation of a transportation museum and the restoration of the Old Santa Fe Railroad Station. "We have a private palace car that we bought which has Victorian tiffany chandeliers and Steuben glass globes, and eighteen other pieces of railroad rolling stock. It will be quite an elaborate program, and for the children who have never traveled by train, it will present so much history."

The development of an extensive railroad exhibit is especially dear to Northen, because the railroad remains one of her favorite means of

136

travel. "I've never flown. My father asked me not to fly and it's my greatest pleasure to do exactly what my father wanted me to do. I think had my father lived a short time longer, he would have changed his mind. But that was just at the beginning of commercial air travel. So I've never flown," Northen says, then adds with a smile, "Well, I went up into the air in a hot air balloon once. But that was just straight up and down, so I didn't really break my father's wishes."

Entering her ninth decade, Northen continues to serve as senior chairman of Moody National Bank and as chairman of the board of trustees of the Moody Foundation, a major philanthropic trust established by her parents in 1942. Northen was one of the three original members of the board, serving with her father and one of his associates, and she has participated in decisions to contribute nearly $90 million to Texas educational institutions, medical centers, cultural and humanitarian organizations. "My parents wanted all of the funds available from the Foundation to be spent only in Texas, so we have tried over the years to always support the things which offer the greatest benefit where there is need. So much has been done already, but there is so much more to do," she firmly states.

Dr. May Owen

Around Ft. Worth, she is known simply as Dr. May—a fixture in the local medical community for so long that few can remember when she was not in her laboratory. Although increasing age has forced a halt to the fifteen-hour days that began her career and continued nearly to the present, she still serves on the staff of three Tarrant County hospitals, is a consulting pathologist for other hospitals, and is a trustee of the Tarrant County Junior College District. The Hall of Health Science of the Ft. Worth Museum of Science and History, a project she promoted by raising funds, giving speeches and twisting arms, was dedicated to her when it opened and bears her name. And the walls of her office at All Saint's Hospital are plastered with awards, some yellow with age, that chronicle her work since she graduated from medical school in 1921 and returned to Texas.

May Owen was born, one of eight children, in Falls County, "on a ranch about twelve miles from nowhere." Her mother died when she was a child, and she grew up, she says, "sort of like Topsy. We were very, very poor. One of my earliest memories is of burning the thorns off cactus to feed the cattle during a drought. We had land, but you couldn't give it away in those days." She decided, by age nine, that she wanted to be a doctor, although she could see no way to finance her dream, which her father sternly opposed.

In her teens she moved to Ft. Worth and worked evenings and weekends to pay her way through the Texas Christian University preparatory school. While earning her undergraduate degree at TCU, Owen worked as a laboratory technician and as an assistant in chemistry to pay her expenses. By eating sparsely, wearing clothes ''until they almost fell apart,'' and walking to the campus from downtown to save the five-cent streetcar fare, May Owen graduated owing him ten dollars. ''And I paid it back the first chance I could,'' she exclaims now. Her frugal ways became ingrained: Her current home is one room, not a luxurious one, in a downtown hotel where she lives, taking her meals in the coffee shop downstairs.

After she graduated from TCU, her application to nursing school was rejected on the grounds that she had excellent grades but no extracurricular activities. While a girl friend was attempting to teach Owen to play tennis, so she would have an activity other than work to place on her next application, May Owen learned that she might enter medical school by first working in a laboratory.

''I got a job with Dr. T. C. Terrell's laboratory. Dr. Terrell said I needed experience, not just what I had learned from books, but that if I was willing to wash baseboards, I could have the job.'' She gave up tennis lessons, and from that time, her occupation became both her work and her pleasure.

Owen was accepted on first application by Louisville Medical College, despite complaints from her classmates. ''The boys didn't want me to be in the class. They went to the dean and said, 'We're not going to accept a woman; we wanted all men.' The dean said, 'It is too late, she's already accepted.' But the boys in my class turned out to be wonderful. I had little money and they were always taking me to the Derby, to the races, for a meal. Now some of the courses, the ones they thought I would never practice, sort of embarrassed them. One of them in particular was male genitalia. They told the dean, 'We'll see that she gets the notes and that she passes the Board. But she'll never need this.' So I took the course on paper, but I was never actually in the classroom.''

After postgraduate work at Bellevue Hospital in New York and at the Mayo Clinic, she returned in 1928 to Terrell's Laboratories in Ft. Worth. ''When I got out of medical school, with all that training, there were surgeons here in town, who would not take my opinion on tissues. I had to split the specimen in half and send part of it to a doctor at Massachusetts General, and after he agreed with me for some time, the surgeons began to believe me. The men who were here before me, they didn't question them as much, but it didn't make me mad. I was glad to be approved. If you think you're right, you're glad to be backed up.

''I've never been mistreated as a woman. The men wanted to make me president of the Tarrant County Medical Society and then the

Texas Medical Association several years before I accepted the positions. I've tried to stay in a woman's place, and I think that's helped me more than anything else. I never tried to force myself on them. I tried to dress like a woman; I didn't smoke and I didn't drink. During medical school, I knew the boys gambled, but I didn't say anything about that. When we were in the bullpen sitting on those bleachers and waiting for the professor to come in and lecture or operate, the boys would gamble before class. I'd stay outside the door and make a noise to let them know the teacher was coming.''

When she returned to Ft. Worth and associated with Terrell's, part of her time was spent helping veterinarians with livestock problems. Her independent research showing that molasses cake, then commonly fed to feed-lot sheep, induced diabetic coma in the animals led to changes in feeding practices. ''I rode these prairies here with the cowboys and veterinarians on Sundays and in the evenings. There were years after medical school when I went to more veterinary meetings than others.''

''I remember one telephone call, on a Sunday a little after midnight. The fellow said, 'I'm coming in from Hillsboro with a mule that might have rabies.' He was in a panic and scared to wait until morning. I got up and got dressed. I was living at the hotel, driving a little Willis-Knight then. I drove over to the laboratory and they rode up with the mule laying in the back of a truck. I had to get the mule's head off and lug it inside. That was an experience. We didn't have any electric saws then. I had to use a meat saw. I finished up around daybreak, and the mule didn't have rabies, so the fellow drove back with it to the rendering plant. I just stayed on and worked at the laboratory the rest of the day.''

In 1936 Owen discovered that talc powder used on surgical gloves sometimes entered wounds, causing adhesions and eventual peritonitis. ''There was a nineteen-year-old girl who had had an appendectomy months earlier. Later, she again had abdominal pain and was operated on, but the surgical opinion of probable tuberculosis could not be confirmed. My boss let me use 120 rabbits to prove that talc powder had caused her problem. I got the powder from several different hospitals and opened the rabbits and sprinkled them with powder. After several months the rabbits were operated on, and the same changes were found in the rabbit tissues as in tissues from patients.'' Her work led powder manufacturers across the country to develop a new absorbable powder. ''I didn't make any money, but it probably saved a number of people from granulomatous peritonitis.'' Her discovery led to an honorary doctorate of science degree from her alma mater.

In the early 1950's when cattle on nearby ranches were dying "by the hundreds," Dr. May would set out in a jeep with veterinarians on weekends and in the evenings after work to inspect affected herds. She concluded from her investigations that oil on the machinery used to cut the cattle feed into pellets was poisoning the animals. "We found it, chloronaphthalene poisoning, but were afraid to publish it. Terrell's was a little firm, and if we'd said what we thought it was, nobody would have listened or believed us." Chemists from the University of Wisconsin arrived at the same conclusion and backed May Owen's findings.

In recent years, she has spent more time as a consultant than as an investigator. In 1976 Dr. Owen spearheaded a drive that resulted in the establishment of a medial school of technology associated with Tarleton State University, which she calls maternally and without bragging "my school." She has funded a chair in pathology at the Texas Tech University Health Sciences Center, and a scholarship in her name has been established in the Ft. Worth area for high-school students interested in the allied health fields.

May Owen never married. But there is a collection of people she calls "my boys and girls," an assortment of nearly two hundred doctors, nurses, medical technologists, two businessmen and a single lawyer whose educations she has helped finance. Most of them are Texans, and May Owen is at her happiest when one or two drop by the coffee shop to accept her standing invitation to join her for Sunday breakfast.

For nearly forty years she has been underwriting future careers. "I've always been on the side of education. It makes so much possible. My boys and girls must be good students and they must show need. They must also be willing to work. I worked my way through school and they're going to work for some of theirs. We don't give them the money outright. We lend it to them. There was one boy I took in grammar school one time, but I don't count that one. I gave him money out of my pocket until he finished medical school, and he worked nights for me.

"But my boys and girls," she continues, "they are loaned the money at a low rate of interest and pay it back when they can. I have a foundation now that takes care of it for me. I used to turn around and write a check when the student dropped by my office. Many of them now have children with Owen as their middle name," she laughs. "I had a batch go in the forties. If I hadn't had a good bookkeeper, I'd have been in trouble. I wouldn't have been able to eat."

One of her "boys," who dedicated his first book to Dr. Owen and refers to her as his second mother, claims that the students she assisted through school assimilated her trait of self-discipline. "Most of us, from working nights and weekends with Dr. Owen while we were in school—and believe me, she worked darn hard and she expected you to—have developed into physicians who love to work. She made us interested in becoming leaders in our particular fields, people who conduct research and who work long, hard hours not for financial promise or for the public's recognition, but because achieving the endeavor is the reward."

Gladys Porter

The personalized license tag for the Cadillac she drives says THE ZOO, and it's a rare day that she doesn't stop, at least for a few minutes, at the Gladys Porter Zoo in Brownsville, which has taken not only her name but also a large portion of her energies.

On cool days, she walks the path of the compact zoo, but during summer months, she slides behind the wheel of a zoo cart to make her rounds. As she talks of the animals and the exotic vegetation, she sounds like a well-informed neighbor: She knows when the tiger is recuperating from a bad tooth or whether the water pressure is strong enough to allow washing down the children's area. After a brief, raucous visit with her favorites, the orangutans, she walks out of the animal enclosure to excited questions from children gathered to watch.

Porter has the soft, grey hair and crinkled laugh lines about her eyes that characterized grandmothers before the advent of Clairol and cosmetic surgery. Dressed in a comfortable pink mu-mu and sensible pumps, she smiles at zoo patrons and appears to be hostessing an informal garden party. Children approach her to ask the names of certain animals or directions to the refreshment stand.

The idea for a zoo came to her in the mid-1960's as she read many articles dealing with the problems of endangered and vanishing species of animals. A zoo would provide refuge for endangered species, she thought, and at the same time accomplish some of her longheld goals for the Brownsville area by providing urban renewal, recreational and educational facilities for the citizens and additional tourist attractions for the city.

Initial discussions began in 1966, and for the next five years Gladys Porter was actively involved in directing the entire dream from drawing board to opening day. At her urging, her family's charitable foundation loaned the city enough funds to pay for the condemned land, thus insuring that families living there would receive adequate funds to relocate. With her further coaxing, the foundation agreed to pay for planning, construction and stocking of the zoo. The foundation continues to make up any deficits in zoo operations.

After the zoo opened in 1971, attendance expectations were exceeded, and the number of visitors continues to surprise zoo officials. Two months after the zoo opened, Gladys Porter was awarded the Governor's Tourist Development award; in 1973 she was presented tha annual Morris Foundation Award for her many contributions to the welfare of animals.

Born in Oklahoma City, Porter studied at Finch College in New York and has been active in community affairs in the Rio Grande Valley since her twenties. She and her husband, Dean Porter, who died in 1969, engaged in ranching and real estate development in Olmito a few miles north of Brownsville. They later moved to Brownsville, where he served one term as mayor, and where most of her philanthropic contributions have been made.

One of Porter's earliest endeavors was the founding of the Brownsville Junior Service League. "I was lucky," she says. "When I came to the Valley, I was young with plenty of energy and this was an area where there was so much to be done. You must remember, there were no government agencies in the thirties doing what they do today. The children were not even TB-tested. Our League gave the children supplemental feedings and innoculations for the childhood diseases that children born in different situations received routinely. That has been taken over by the government now, but for a long time, we provided a service that was sorely lacking in the community. The government has taken over so many things that there's little left for the volunteer to do now but record keeping. I think volunteer effort and private enterprise can accomplish more, but there's little an individual can say now to stop government."

A letter in 1946 from her father, Earl C. Sams, who served many years as president and later chairman of the board of the J. C. Penney Company, cautioned her that "Great wealth also conveys great responsibility." Not long after, the Earl C. Sams Foundation was formed and funded. Through this foundation, which Porter has directed since her father's death, stadiums have been erected, Girl Scout camps established, Boy's Clubs funded, college buildings financed, and hospital wings furnished.

"We have tried to focus on community needs that might not be met if government or civic agencies were left to do them. And many of the things we've accomplished couldn't have been done except through private enterprise. There are so many different projects competing for the public dollar. Private contribution often does the extras which make life richer. Brownsville couldn't have afforded this kind of place," she says, sweeping her hand toward the carefully manicured zoo walkways. Porter's diverse philanthropic activities earned her the title "Miss South Texas" in 1975, although many people still call her "that zoo lady," referring to her most visible project.

Beyond her knowledge of the problems and habits of most of the animals, Porter has developed an awareness of the zoo as a business institution. As president of the Valley Zoological Society, which directs operations of the zoo, she is constantly researching new methods for increasing public financial support. One popular idea was an adoption program in which individuals would support a zoo "child" for a year. Her son-in-law found himself supporting a rhinoceros for twelve months. Not everyone is willing to feed a mouth that size. "Our grocery orders range from potatoes and carrots and beef to the exotic products which must come from zoo suppliers. And we must feed the animals, no matter what is happening to food costs. You can't very well tell a Siberian tiger that he will have to begin a vegetarian diet!" she says.

Porter follows the voluminous paperwork that is required before animals are introduced to their Brownsville homes. "It's a long, expensive process. The animals are kept in quarantine in Mombassa before they are shipped. Then most of them come air cargo and must remain in New Jersey in quarantine for a sixty-day period before they can come to our zoo. With the food and care the animals get for those months, it is like keeping them in expensive hotels!"

In the first years of the zoo's existence, Porter accompanied zoo officials on several catching safaris, an experience she recalls as "a rugged adventure. I just wanted to see the countryside, the natural habitat, and the animals in their environment. And I wanted to know just how the hunting was done. It was an exciting experience, but I don't know that I'd ever do it again," she laughs. But even if she doesn't hunt rare animals in the wild any more, she will continue to hunt another rare species, someone willing to support a hungry rhinoceros for yet another year.

Gladys Porter died, following a brief illness, on March 26, 1980, during preparation of this book.

Lorene Rogers

During the thick of protest over her appointment as president of the University of Texas, Dr. Lorene Rogers walked briskly across the campus one morning in her "Buck Rogers" tee shirt. With the proverbial eyes of Texas on her, it was a confident action, but she has never been short on confidence. A few years earlier, when she was told, during an official visit to the Air Force Academy, that she would not be allowed to dine with her male colleagues in the cadet dining room, she gathered her luggage and briefcase and caught the next available flight for Texas.

"I think just growing up in Texas gives you confidence. There is a 'can do' spirit in Texas that helps. The other thing that had an effect on me was my mother. She was a shy, retiring kind of person, but she was the strength of our family." As a preschooler in tiny Prosper, Texas, Rogers would walk a mile or so to the store on errands for her mother, stopping to talk with the townsfolk as she went. ". . . that kind of experience gave me confidence early in the game," she recalls.

Rogers has been described by critics as, at best, cold and even by friends as reserved. Yet, when she takes time out and talks about her career at UT, she is surprisingly warm. It appears at first that she prefers to avoid talk of her private life, angling conversation at every opportunity back to the University. Instead, it becomes apparent that for many years her personal life and her professional life have been fused.

Valedictorian of her high-school class, Rogers was the first member of her family to attend college. About her freshman year at North Texas State Teacher's College in Denton, she says, "I didn't know what I was going to do . . . I happened to get into this class with an outstanding English teacher who convinced me to major in English." She signed up for chemistry only to meet the science requirement. During the first or second class, the elderly professor, demonstrating the activity of sodium, placed some sodium in a beaker of water; it popped out all over him and the front-row students. "I walked out and dropped the class and took geology and biology for my science," Rogers recalls.

Despite this inauspicious introduction to chemistry, Rogers became interested in the subject after marrying a chemist and listening to him and his colleagues discuss their research. Soon after her sixth wedding anniversary, her husband died following an injury he sustained in a laboratory accident at the New Jersey chemical plant where he worked. With no chemistry courses to her credit, Lorene Rogers, at age twenty-seven, returned to Austin to enroll in the chemistry department at the University of Texas. Five years later she received her master's degree in organic chemistry and had completed the requirements for a doctorate in biochemistry.

At one point during her graduate studies Rogers was offered a position as a teaching assistant but refused it when she learned that her salary would be half that given to a male student in the same position. "The professor really didn't think women belonged where I was, but he was honest and had given me the grade that I made. I was the only one who made an A. But when I asked, 'Why are you paying me half what you've been paying the men?' he said 'I may have to help you.' I said, 'Sir, did you help me make the grade in your course last year?' He said 'No, but there might be some lifting to do.' So, he taught the course himself rather than give me the salary . . . ."

After serving as a full professor in chemistry at Sam Houston State College for a year, Dr. Rogers returned in late 1949 to UT's Clayton Foundation Biochemical Institute as a research scientist. Told when she arrived that she would probably be appointed to the chemistry faculty when a vacancy appeared, she was still waiting for that event more than a decade later. While serving as assistant director of the Institute, Rogers turned down more lucrative positions from corporations and more prestigious positions from other universities. She had a tenacious desire to remain at the University of Texas, despite the professional or financial cost. When she was offered a professorship in nutrition at another university in 1962, the director of the Institute began to actively push for her placement on the UT chemistry faculty, she recalls. These efforts were met with a blanket refusal, and the selection committee's response was "Absolutely not. We know her, we like her, we respect her, but she's a woman and we don't intend to have a woman on this faculty," Rogers says.

"I thought it was a stupid reason, but this was so much the case in so many major schools at that time . . . . I guess the other reason I didn't resent it more than I did was that I was interested in research and I wanted to be in a good school. I could have had a professorship if I had settled for a lesser school."

The issue was resolved when Rogers accepted a "half-time" position as professor of nutrition in the department of home economics, retaining her position in the Biochemical Institute. While in the nutrition department she directed research on the effects of nutritional deficiencies and drugs on the cause of congenital malformations.

"I had not been eligible for academic administrative positions until I was on the faculty, and in 1964, out of the blue, the graduate dean called me and asked if I would consider being an associate dean. Because, in part, no woman had ever had that kind of job before on this campus or on any other major campus in the nation, I decided that I ought to give it a try and see whether it could be done."

When she was later named vice-president of the University in 1971, one of her first jobs was to serve as the Chairman of the Committee on the Status of Women within the University. "We got a number of things straightened out. I do not claim that complete justice was done, but the situation was much better by the end of the year than it was at the beginning of the year. We have continued this of course. There is a standing committee of students, faculty and staff on the status of women and minorities, and an Equal Employment Opportunity Officer who sees to it when there are faculty positions open, for example, that women are considered right along with the men. If the man is employed and the woman isn't, reasons have to be given why the difference was made. Also, after the budget is done each year, it's examined to see if any women's salaries appear to be out of line."

When Stephen Spurr was dismissed from the presidency in 1974, the fifth president in six years, Dr. Rogers was named interim president of the University. During the following year the Board of Regents tried repeatedly to find a new president acceptable to the faculty, staff and students. "There were two different committees, one was supposed to be the selection committee and the other, the advisory. The advisory committee never accepted the fact that it was advisory. It wanted to be the one to name the president. And those two committees were like this the whole time," Rogers says, placing her two clenched fists against each other.

"I did most of my wondering if the presidency was worth it ahead of time. The chairman of the Board of Regents came to me two or three days before I was named and asked me if I would take it. I did all of my struggling during the next two days. Finally, when he came back two days later, I told him that the answer was no. I said 'I told you all here that I didn't want the job under the best of circumstances and I certainly don't want it under these.' We talked more, and I told him 'If you want me to take it, don't name me tomorrow. The regents are leaving the next day. Wait until the next meeting of the Board and let's just do some further thinking about this.' He went away and I thought that was settled. Then, that night about 9 o'clock, I was contacted and they said that things were just getting completely out of hand and they had to name a president.''

The vote was five to three and Rogers was surprised when some members of the Board of Regents, including Lady Bird Johnson, voted against her appointment. "I had recognized that there would be differences of opinion when they were in executive session, but I had thought that they would come out and vote unanimously. It would have made my job much easier.

"During the first day or two, I was not certain the job was going to get to me or not, because the protesting was escalating all the time. I had been invited before this took place to go to the White House and watch President Ford present the National Medals of Science. I decided to go at the last minute, and it turned out to be the best thing I could have done. I got away for a few days, and I got a different perspective. After I came back I never had a moment's doubt that I was going to do it. They could do whatever they wanted to, and I was going to do the job. And we had a very successful year that first year.''

The major problems facing higher education in the next few years, Rogers says, are both the lack of confidence of the public and the Proposition 13 syndrome, which she sees as a threat to educational funding. "We lost the public confidence during the student protest days and we're gradually gaining it back because the student population has changed. They're very serious and career minded. I did all that I could to keep things on an even keel on campus. You do this by trying to be fair to everybody, having reasons for what you've done, giving reasons. As long as things are going well then we have a chance of regaining the public confidence. In a school like Texas, you have to have the confidence of the public because we get our appropriations from the legislature . . . . Without public confidence, we are all in trouble.''

As president of the University, social commitments kept Rogers up many nights a week. For relaxation after working a long day, she would turn to solitary pastimes, such as reading, playing the piano, working crossword puzzles in the *Saturday Review*. There were no golf clubs or tennis racquets in her closets, no bridge dates marked on her appointment calendar. Although Rogers has traveled to more than two dozen countries during the past thirty years, she has done so not as a tourist but as an advisor, a representative, or a committee member for a host of educational organizations. In addition to the meetings she attended as president of UT, Rogers often performed the duties usually reserved for a president's wife, entertaining students and faculty wives at social gatherings.

All of this activity ended when Rogers reached retirement age and stepped down as president in August 1979. For the first time in several decades, the transition from one president to another occurred smoothly as Rogers and the new president, Dr. Peter Flawn, met regularly to assure the transition of power. Although Rogers had planned to spend her retirement working on her Austin home, gardening, relaxing and enjoying her unscheduled hours, she received several job offers by the fall of 1979. "I may not take any of them. I have my home here, my friends here, but it certainly makes me feel good to have them offered."

Like all die-hard Texas Exes, Dr. Rogers can talk for hours about the many accomplishments of diverse segments of "THE" University. It amuses her that she attended the presentation of the Heisman Trophy to a UT student one evening and left the following morning for Sweden to see a faculty member receive his Nobel Prize. But when Lorene Rogers talks about the University of Texas, she is talking simultaneously about her life, for the two were closely intertwined for thirty years; it will probably take several years before Rogers can look at the UT tower jutting into the Austin skyline without thinking, momentarily, that she has appointments to keep.

Gloria Scott

A favorite story told often by Gloria Scott tells a lot about her philosophy. As the story goes, a pig and a hen were walking down a street lined with breakfast shops. They were surprised at the low prices being charged for bacon and eggs, and although the hen concluded the low cost must be fair, the pig was distressed. "For you to give two eggs is just a contribution on your part," the pig exclaimed. "But for me to give bacon, I have to make a total commitment!"

In describing her own experiences as a youngster, and later as national president of the Girl Scouts, a teacher and college administrator, Scott often recounts anecdotes with a grin and laugh. When she talks about her commitment to equality, social justice and quality education, she emerges as a determined woman who recognized early the value of planning, goals, accomplishment.

"I've never been one to sit on the sidelines. . . . If you want to affect policy and see your ideas implemented, you have to do more than sit in your own living room and talk about it." And she has consciously chosen to commit herself as a volunteer. "I believe that in the long run the private volunteer sector has the greatest impact on our lives. Lots of people suggested to me that I seek Barbara Jordan's seat when she decided not to run again for Congress. But I'm an independent; I vote for the person whose basic attitudes or positions I can support. . . . Most people who get involved in volunteering are not motivated by personal gain. You get involved because you have an idea that you really want to succeed. There is something about political life where you have trade-offs, red tape. It is often hard to keep sight of the goals.''

Her own deep commitment to education and the advancement of minorities and women had her working double time for three years in the 1970's. When the Girl Scouts of the USA elected her president in 1975, the first time in its long history that a black woman had been chosen, Gloria Scott accepted the time-consuming volunteer position while maintaining her full-time position as assistant to the president at Texas Southern University in Houston.

Scott, a petite and vivacious woman, was occasionally mistaken for a young troop member during the years that she worked with the Scouts regularly. But once she rose to speak from behind a podium, even if that meant standing balanced on boxes, there was no mistaking her maturity. Chosen to head the Girl Scouts at a time when participation was declining, minorities were underrepresented, and charges were being levied that the organization was no longer relevant to contemporary life, Scott made an all-out effort to change these trends. During her presidency, the National Council endorsed support for the Equal Rights Amendment to the dismay of some, the applause of others. At her installation ceremony, a vote was taken on whether to admit boys to membership, and Scott was pleased when the measure failed to gain support.

"Young men have traditionally had so many support groups. With all the team sports and things like their own scouting organization, boys have had an opportunity to learn to work together, to develop leadership and organizational skills. For young women, until very recently, most activities were of an individual nature. And while girls learned many things, they often did not have the opportunity to learn the skills of working within an organization, skills that are very important to them later.''

Her belief in organizations and collective action runs deep and has been a key to her own success. In scouting, religious groups, her college sorority and academic groups, Scott has worked within the framework of an organization. "I won't say that the individual cannot accomplish anything. But I believe that the group is what helps to move people along and accomplish worthwhile goals. Women are beginning to recognize the value of encouraging and supportive groups—something men have realized for a long time.''

As a child, Scott was encouraged by her family and by an early teacher. Her father was a Houston restaurant cook; her mother, a domestic worker; and both parents emphasized studies to Scott. "My

156

mother is a bright woman who was offered a chance to go to college by her father and decided not to go. She was always reading and encouraging me to read as a child. Years later, when I was in high school, my mother made the decision to become a licensed practical nurse. Because we needed the money, she knew that she would always have to work. So she decided that she would learn to do something that she could enjoy and that would be fulfilling and worthwhile. After working all day, she went to classes at night until she was licensed.''

The middle of five children, Scott was enrolled at a neighborhood church kindergarten when she was four and left for first grade at age five as the valedictorian of her kindergarten class. ''My first-grade teacher was very important. She was a young widow who took the time to take us on field trips, invite us to her home. She made me believe there were many things I could do with my life if I prepared myself with a sound education. And she was very dark skinned. That was important because, particularly at that time, we had a caste system in the black community based on color. Most of the teachers were lighter skinned, . . . So to have a very dark teacher, who was also a very capable and respected teacher, was valuable. She was a wonderful role model.''

A later role model, Scott says, was future congresswoman Barbara Jordan. ''I remember, as a young teen, when she [Barbara Jordan] was chosen 'Girl of the Year' as a senior at Phillis Wheatley High School. It was a really big honor, and I told myself that in a few years I would perhaps be 'Girl of the Year' at Jack Yates High School were I went to school. Then, the year I think I would have received the award, the administration discontinued it. I was crushed!'' Scott laughs now.

As a little girl, Scott longed to join the group of classmates who weekly wore their Girl Scout uniforms to school. But she and her family assumed, wrongly she later learned, that scouting would cost too much for the family's tight budget. Scott became a Y-ette instead, but when she was fourteen, with money earned from babysitting and from an after-school job at a drug store, she became a Girl Scout. In 1954, when she was sixteen, Scott attended her first state convention, in Austin, and she recalls, ''That was one of the first times that I had a clear picture about segregation. The black girls stayed at a black campus and the white girls stayed at the University of Texas campus. We had gone together as one group from Houston, and part of the discussion at the meetings was on black and white Scouts working together. But there was systematic segregation in the city; that was the world at the time. It didn't ruin my trip though. My best friend and I went to see the state capitol and paid a visit to the Secretary of State—uninvited,'' she laughs, before continuing. ''I saw scouting as a ray of hope, because scouting was based on the idea that a Girl Scout is a sister to all other Scouts. It was one of the few organizations that offered mixing of the races, encouraged with exchange of ideas.''

When the time came to attend college, Scott looked north. ''The University of Texas was beginning to desegregate, but I was a serious student and I didn't want to have to handle all the problems that I knew would come with a school in its early days of desegregation. I also wanted to go to another part of the country to see how things were there. And I felt some bitterness that the University of Texas hadn't desegregated before then.'' She attended the University of Indiana on an academic scholarship and, encouraged by the love of nature she had developed as a Scout, received her bachelor's and her master's degree in zoology. Later, after her career goals changed, she earned a doctorate in college and university administration in 1965.

Scott's plans to marry late, after her career was established, were altered when she met Will Braxton Scott at the University of Indiana. Of her decision to marry, Scott says, ''I always knew I was going to have a career and some personal independence. Will was a few years older . . . and certainly more mature than any of my peers, and he recognized and respected my goals.'' Although the Scotts have no children of their own, their home has rarely been without a live-in college student, making college affordable for a student who otherwise would not be able to attend.

After her husband had returned to school and completed his doctorate in sociology, the Scotts traveled together, holding jobs at the same colleges and universities. Teaching positions and academic administrative posts have taken them from Indiana to Texas, Tennessee, North Carolina and Georgia, where Gloria Scott accepted a position as vice-president of Clark College in 1978.

Since she first began teaching in 1961, Scott has seen many ''gradual but real'' changes in the attitudes of young women on college campuses. ''In 1961, young women were not seeing where they could go. It was still part of the 'feminine mystique' era. I've seen young women move from the idea that you go to college to get a husband to the knowledge that there are choices to be made in life. . . .

''I think it's still harder for chicano and black women who are trying to succeed. Within the chicano or black community there are parallel opportunities, but to move into the mainstream is more difficult. And there are two conflicting groups, racial and women, vying for their attention. I have people ask me how I can be concerned with women's issues. I say that everything I do is involved in being black. They are not in isolation. It means a heavier burden on the energies of minority women because you are at one and the same time part of two minorities.''

Educational and career opportunities have taken the Scotts far from their native state, although many of their vacations are spent fishing and waterskiing at their waterfront cabin in Riviera, Texas. But like her grandparents and great-grandparents, who came from Tennessee and Alabama at the time of the end of slavery, Scott believes Texas is a "place of opportunity. There is a Texas mystique," she says, "something that began back then, and continues today. It has to do with space. . . . As a child, even a poor child in the city, you had more space than children in other cities. Nearly everyone had a house. And when you read and learned about the state's history, there was a kind of adventure in action and spirit, a quality of personal determination that continues to the present."

For Gloria Scott, personal determination and a sense of adventure and spirit have forged a commitment that propelled her from the sidelines into action, seeking equality, social justice and quality education.

160

Jaclyn Smith

She walks with the grace of a dancer down the stairs and into her parents' living room in Houston. A book balanced on her head would not fall. Thin, more petite than she appears on a television screen, Jaclyn Smith looks like the mythical Texas beauty sprung to life, lady-like in man-cut trousers and a bulky turtleneck sweater.

In her role as Kelly on *Charlie's Angels,* Smith may capture thieves, wisecrack beguilingly and appear to be the got-it-together woman of recent years. But away from the set and constant coddling of makeup experts, she seems the prototype of the old-fashioned girl. She is a woman who says, while earning fortunes on her own, ''I like a man who runs the house and takes care of you. A man you can turn to and ask, 'Hey, is everything going to be all right?' And he says, 'Everything is going to be all right.' ''

Having invested her earnings and formed her own production company, Smith sees little reason to become involved with women's groups. ''I believe in equal pay, but in my business I've never felt I've been mistreated. I'd stand up for women who have been, but I wouldn't feel passionate about the movement. I believe in men opening doors and taking care of the woman. I think with the movement, a lot of times, it takes femininity away and the men stop being the powerful figure.''

Her voice is soft, practically bereft of any Texas influence. And when she talks about things that anger her, like being forced to leave her hotel by a side door to avoid pursuing photographers on her wedding day, she resorts to expletives that most people abandoned for fiercer vocabulary in the fifth grade.

When she is not working, Smith spends much of her time decorating her eighteenth-century, colonial-style home in California. She works almost every weekend with disadvantaged children and still fosters a long-time dream of opening a dance school for underprivileged youngsters. She does not enjoy the constant hovering of makeup specialists and hair stylists when she is filming, so spare hours are spent without makeup, running in the park with her dogs and relaxing with her husband, actor Dennis Cole.

Smith talks in matter-of-fact, business-like tones of her career. But when she speaks of her family, and especially of her late maternal grandfather, Gaston Hartfield, her voice grows warm and enthusiastic. Some of her fondest memories are of trips to the family farm in Luling with family friends and relatives.

During visits with her family in Houston, Smith goes out of her way to avoid attention and stays mostly at home. "Mother does have a hard time turning children away; she has lots of twelve-year-old friends now," Smith laughs, whispering to explain that the occasional, shrill giggles from the Smith kitchen are from three elementary-school girls waiting to present her with a fresh-baked chocolate cake. Smith savors such private family hours, and at the end of a visit she returns to the airport not in a chauffeured limosine but in her father's car so that the two of them can prolong her stay until the plane boards.

As a high-school student, Smith was more interested in dancing than dating, and she can remember times when she felt like a wallflower. "I was so totally involved with ballet and with school productions. And I had such definite ideas about things. I didn't really fit into the popular crowd that wore Pappagalo shoes, shirtwaists and circle pins."

Smith began studying ballet when she was three years old, and by the time she was twelve, she had decided to pursue a career in dance. After a year at Trinity College in San Antonio, she left for New York City. "I was a very good dancer, but emotionally I didn't have the stamina or the dedication. George Balanchine takes dancers at the age of twelve and molds them, their minds and their bodies, into dancers. I had the motions, but not the drive." She turned to commercials and off-Broadway theater productions. During this period, Smith married and gave up her career for almost four years. "It's just as well, it wasn't time lost. I probably needed all that time to adjust to what goes into this type of career. Believe me, it's a discipline."

Paramount Pictures put her under an option contract which led to classes in voice and acting and to small roles in television and films.

"My career was moving, slowly, but it was going," Smith recalls. "I wasn't making tremendous money, but I was working regularly . . . . I had been working for over ten years, but when *Charlie's Angels* went over, people thought I was an instant hit."

Although her contract with ABC and *Charlie's Angels* runs until 1981, she will be glad when her part in the series ends. "It has stopped being a challenge. I hate to sound ungrateful because it has made everything else possible. And I owe it to the show to stick it out until the end, but it's a hard job. The Angels are really like Barbie Dolls. They don't say too much, just smile a lot. We've tried to develop unique characters, but we're not given that much time to act. It's 'Hold-it-freeze-are-you-okay-freeze-smile-freeze.' "

Her parents never miss a program. "Criticize the show? Are you kidding? They think it's *Gone With the Wind.* In fact, they watch all the repeats, the third time around. But then, my parents criticize very little I've done."

Smith continues to study privately with an acting coach, preparing herself for roles that she hopes will demand more from her. She will follow her agent's advice, she says, and surround herself with box office stars when she makes a film, "rather than taking a movie by myself like Farrah did. I was surprised with Farrah. I thought her movie *Somebody Killed Her Husband* would do well. I didn't see it, but it closed so quickly. I don't know what went wrong, unless people resented her leaving *Charlie's Angels.*" Smith has formed her own company, GH Productions, which is named for her grandfather, a Methodist minister; it appears likely that any film she produces would have passed her grandfather's moral approval.

"My grandfather was the strong person in my background. He was always concerned for other people, and he was never self-righteous or stern . . . . he always talked patiently and answered any question I asked. He never made fun or teased me. He made me feel important. We'd just talk as we were driving to San Marcos or Waco or wherever we were going. It was totally opposite from my life now; the simplicity as opposed to all the commotion. I'm happy now, but I'm glad I have those days to look back on. When things get overpowering and a bit superficial, it's good to look back and see that warm relationships and friends and caring are what it is all about."

Although her grandfather died several years ago, most of the thoughts that Smith writes in her journal are still about him, she says. "My family certainly didn't push me toward an acting career. They only encouraged me to do whatever I wanted to do. I think my grandfather would have been tickled to see me marry and move right next door to my mother."

Sissy Spacek

She answers the door herself, wearing her sweatshirt, painter's pants and scuffed cowboy boots—a salesman might well ask for her mother. As a slice of grin appears, she becomes an image of pixiness. Despite her youthful appearance and informality, Sissy Spacek has already earned an Oscar nomination, film critics' praise and cover stories for her portrayals of intense, young southern waifs.

Spacek grew up in Quitman, Texas, and like most small-town residents, she still knows many of the fifteen hundred or so people who live in the town. She lives now in the Topanga Canyon area of Los Angeles but returns as often as possible, often for months at a time, to the log cabin that she and her husband have purchased five miles outside of Quitman. It is a rural area of the state, ninety miles northeast of Dallas in the Piney Woods, which some writers have called a territory of unformed character, Texas' last regional identity crisis. But Spacek credits the innocence of the land and the naturalness of its people with the inspiration that she draws upon to create new characters upon the screen.

Born on Christmas Day in 1950, she was an all-American girl as she grew up: Mary Elisabeth Spacek the cheerleader, rodeo contestant, baton twirler, 4-H club member, homecoming queen and beauty contestant, who looked sweet but never won the crown. After graduation, she might have gone on to college and sorority life like many of her friends, except that her older brother lay dying of leukemia as she entered her senior year. His death, she recalls, "changed everything . . . It gives you a glimpse. It lets you know there might not be as much time as you thought."

After graduation she left for New York to visit her father's nephew, Rip Torn, and Torn's wife, Geraldine Page, both established actors. "I was hoping some of the success might be inherited," she says. "I was flying standby, and it was the July fourth weekend. There must have been 20,000 soldiers at Love Field waiting to get on, and since service people can get first, it took me three days of staying at the airport, getting bumped off flights, before I ever got out. And when I got off the plane in New York, it was so weird. You know the part of Texas I come from, when you talked long distance, you talked loud and fast. So we hadn't traveled much. No one was there in New York to meet me. Rip had rented a car and driven to the airport three days earlier. You know what a big deal that is in New York. He had met every flight from Texas for two and a half days! I took a taxi and I really tried hard, like my mother had told me, not to let the driver know I didn't know my way around."

She arrived wearing a flowerprint suit and white patent-leather shoes, beaming an elfin smile and trying, she says, not to exclaim at the towering buildings as she approached Manhattan. Several days later, she strummed her twelve-string guitar and sang for dark-suited executives at the William Morris Agency. "They listened a little while and then got together and talked real low. Then they told me to get some more experience." She embellishes her oft told tale of early days in New York with theatrical gestures and wide-eyed exclamations.

Spacek pursued her music career, strumming her guitar in coffee-houses and working as a studio musician. She recorded an album under the stage name of "Rainbo" but that led to no gold records. "At one point I reached a stage when I was so cool, so groovy, I was sitting around all those little tables you can find in New York, saying things like 'far out man, just far out.' And it finally dawned on me that it wasn't for me."

Spacek then made the rounds with her portfolio seeking work as a model. She has a difficult time recalling when her first break came. "My first break was getting invited to New York. No. My first break was when I was born," she laughs. Her first acting opportunity came when she was cast in the role of the young white slave in *Prime Cut*. "When I first saw myself on the screen in that movie, I didn't think, 'Oh, you really made it' or that it was a good or bad movie. I just thought, 'You created a character and you were able to be convincing.'"

Although she studied for eight months with the Lee Strasberg Theatrical Institute, Spacek relies more upon instinct and intuition in her acting than on studied technique. "Sometimes I take a class here and there, if someone special is coming in from New York. And I've done a couple of sessions at an experimental school. Through work, I've acquired a bit of my own technique," she says.

Spacek can regulate the Texas twang in her voice, but when she is relaxed, the Texas influence is pronounced. "One of the first managers I met in New York, who was also from Texas, said, 'Honey, you git rid of that accent, or you just git on back home.' But being from Texas has helped me a lot, emotionally, and so it has helped my career. Growing up there was great. The life I had was wonderful and I got to excel in a lot of things in this little town and I was real involved. I was always proud about being from Texas and, you know, maybe that was part of my fearlessness. I love the fact that Texas is so big, but you don't feel small because of that.

"In the beginning, I can remember thinking I wanted to become just like everybody else in New York. I remember once I was sitting with some friends in my apartment. I was twenty-one. I had just gotten back from Texas, and I'd been gone about two months. I came back and I remember saying something about 'Oh gosh, it was so wonderful. It was like being in hog heaven.' And my friends went 'WHAT! What did you say?' And I thought, 'What did I say that was so awful, so horrible?' Well, they all started to laugh and I got embarrassed and I started to cry. Because 'hog heaven' to them was just hysterical. Now I'm glad for all those differences. It's weird how you fight a lot of that stuff. You know, you want to be like everybody else and something's holding you back until you kind of just find your own place."

Her role in 1973 as the innocent, tag-along accomplice on a murder spree in *Badlands* finally convinced Spacek that she was not a fly-by-night actress, that she would have an acting career. "I was lucky to get that part. I probably wouldn't have gotten it if I hadn't been a Texan. Terrence Malick was the director and he is a Texan. Here I was a little twerp from Texas, and I was able to relate to this young, brilliant man. He was a Rhodes scholar. But we had the same things in common, and we knew about the same Texas experiences. We had a real ability to communicate." Spacek met her husband, art director Jack Fisk, on that film and life from that point on is measured not by calendar years but by film release dates.

After *Badlands,* Spacek turned down many movie roles for nearly two years and worked with her husband as a set designer while she waited for the right property to come along. In 1976 she played a maid in *Welcome to L.A.,* but the film was not released for a year after it was completed. The next script Spacek chose was *Carrie* in which she played an adolescent whom everyone taunted, an innocent who revenged herself on prom night by unleasing telekinetic devastation in the high-school gym. To prepare for the role, she did some soul searching about her friendship with a ''misfit'' at her own high school. ''People used to make fun of her. She was from a poor family and wore strange clothes and kept her distance. I had tried to become friends with her to know what she was like, and I based a lot of the character on her. Then I also studied a lot of Dore etchings of religious sufferings. And I read about telekinesis.''

Her portrayal in *Carrie* earned Spacek the 1976 National Society of Film Critics Award for Best Actress and an Oscar nomination. It also earned her front place in a celebration parade in Quitman. ''I had been traveling in Europe but I had come back to Texas to lead the parade. I was sick and I was getting B-12 shots and everything. But I couldn't not ride on that magnificent palomino.''

After finishing *Carrie*, Spacek made a few television appearances; played a leading role in *3 Women*, which director Robert Altman had written with Spacek and fellow Texan Shelley Duvall in mind; and continued to read and reject many scripts. She chooses her roles carefully, seeking parts that will test her ability, stretch her talent, demand deeper concentration and a wider range of emotions. As Loretta Lynn in *Coal Miner's Daughter*, Spacek played the determined country music star from her marriage at age thirteen through her struggle to stardom and the eventual emotional collapse that success brought at age thirty-five. In *Heart Beat*, based on the life of beat novelist Jack Kerouac, she portrayed a woman, from youth through middle age, who was married to one man but companion to two. Spacek was pleased, after several years of portraying girls, for a chance to finally portray women.

''I am not like any of those people I play. But in order to play them properly, I have to draw upon elements of my own personal experiences so I can relate—so an audience can then relate to me. That's what I mean about an actress being her own tool. And you can't turn down interesting parts because they are too small or you fear the public won't like you in the part. If that's the price of stardom, then it's like the tail wagging the dog.''

Although she thinks the number of roles for women in films is increasing, Spacek also believes ''there's more exploitation of women now. It's in a different way. I don't mean like sex pictures, but now, women are 'in.' It's 'Make a woman's film.' It's still hard to find a good role. I think there are probably more good men's roles still.''

Spacek is not active in political organizations but supports the Equal Rights Amendment and donated all her old scripts and an old

Carrie dress to an auction benefiting ratification efforts. ''I'm thrilled that they got the extension. . . . WE got the extension, excuse me.''

Sissy Spacek seems a little amused, but not at all embarrassed, by the naivete with which she first started her career. ''I left for New York with no idea of how I was going to do it. You know, ignorance must be bliss. I just didn't know about the big odds against me. I didn't realize that everybody else was trying to get into show business. I just knew I wanted it very much.''

Annette Strauss

Upstairs in her North Dallas home, in an attic where extra clothing, furniture and accessories are sorted and stored with more organization than department stores give to their showrooms, Annette Strauss has a closet full of skeletons. Boxes, filing cabinets and shopping bags, all filled with the skeletal framework of more than thirty years of fund-raising efforts, line the floors and shelves. Strauss has been a zealous Dallas volunteer since 1946 and has helped raise enough money to qualify her for the title "Six-Million-Dollar Woman."

Annette Strauss' earliest volunteer effort in Dallas was with the Council of Jewish Women, and she credits the well-structured program there with laying the groundwork for future community endeavors. When she realized that with careful scheduling of her time she could do more, she expanded her volunteer work to include additional cultural and civic programs. Hours were spent addressing envelopes, decorating for benefits, and following orders. "I was a lot of Indians before I was ever a chief, and I seemed to learn something new with each job. I'm a great believer in the old adage that 'God gave us two eyes and two ears and one mouth for a very good reason.'"

As a chief, Strauss has been president of the National Women's Association of Symphony Orchestras and of more than a dozen other groups; she has also served as a director for a wide range of organizations—educational, medical, religious, cultural, business and civic. During the past several years she has headed TACA, Inc., an umbrella organization that funds several of the major arts organizations in Dallas. Serving on the Dallas Park and Recreation Board, she has tried to bring cultural performances to the parks and has worked in outreach programs to take the arts to neighborhoods whose residents have few opportunities to enjoy them. And she has pursued her joint interest in maintaining a vital downtown and restoring the Majestic Theater while serving as a member of the executive committee of the Central Business District Association.

Annette Strauss surprised many in the Dallas community in early 1978 when she decided to enter the paid work force and became the director of public affairs for a local public relations firm. The move didn't mean that she was giving up her dedication to civic and cultural endeavors, only that she will organize a little more and work a little harder. ''My firm is very understanding and knows that my involvement in the community only makes me more valuable to them,'' she says. Although the Strauss balance sheet is not greatly affected by her salary, Annette Strauss likes knowing that her talents are worthy of a paycheck, that the organizational skills she has so carefully honed in the past thirty years are valued in the employment market.

''I'm an organized person and early in life I was taught not to take responsibilities lightly. I give meticulous attention to important details that can make a difference,'' she says. ''I try to do what I say I'll do and try to not worry about the things over which I have no control. My past mistakes have taught me a lot. In any project I set certain goals, try to anticipate things that could go wrong and correct those problems before they happen. I'm a great list maker—purposeful lists that seem to make it a lot easier to get the things done that ought to be done. And then, of course, I pray a lot.''

An only child, Strauss was born in Houston, and her fund-raising talents were developed in childhood. ''I was raising sixty cents to buy chocolate ice cream when I was six years old. I would get some of my friends together and we would do skits on my porch and charge five cents admission,'' Strauss says laughingly as she remembers asking her girlfriends to dress as boys in the chorus while she starred in makeup and a frilly dress as the singing and dancing female lead. ''I was fund raising for the arts when I was six years old—and I found out it was 'nice' to be the leader, even then.''

She attended Rice University for a year, then transferred to the University of Texas at Austin where she was chosen a campus beauty, served in student government and was elected to Phi Beta Kappa. She also met her future husband, Theodore Strauss of Stamford, Texas, but she waited to marry until she had completed her master's work in sociology and psychology at Columbia University, receiving summa cum laude honors. When she moved to Dallas, at age twenty-two, she resumed the volunteer work that she had begun during her teen years with the Red Cross in Houston.

At the same time, her husband was working for Dallas radio station KIXL and had taken on an additional dawn show, ''Poor Old Ted,'' to earn an extra seven dollars a week. ''Keeping a sponsor for the show depended on postcard questions sent in by listeners, so I used to drive around to different parts of the city and mail in postcards for Ted every day,'' she says. Their joint efforts ended successfully: Strauss went on to purchase the radio station and is now Chairman of the Board of Strauss Broadcasting Company. He is also chairman of the board of First City Bank in Dallas and a director of First City Bancorporation of Texas, Inc.

A seasoned volunteer advised Strauss, early in her volunteer career, ''Honey, never forget, there's a nitch for every bitch,'' and although Strauss remembers initial shock at the choice of words, the point was well taken. ''There are always enough people around who want to do volunteer work. Some may just want to work an afternoon or two and lick envelopes. And that's fine; their contribution is important and appreciated. And others want to expend more effort and perform leadership roles. Some only want to give money and attend benefits and don't feel they can do more. They are all important and provide the kind of teamwork that makes for success. It's a question of putting the right person with the right project at the right time.

''Although I have a great deal of feeling for people, much of what I know now, I had to learn through trial and error—but I HAVE learned. I know that there are those who say they will do something and they will often do more. They're the energizers and they make life a lot more fun. And there are those who are equally well intended when they say they will do something, but they just can't. And unfortunately, there are the strength sappers who say they will do something and they never had any intention of doing it. They don't make life more fun and I avoid them when I can.''

In the course of her many projects, from chairing the Women's Division of the United Fund to the elite Crystal Charity Ball, Strauss has compiled lists of which volunteers are best at selling tickets, at getting contributions, at organizing teams of workers, at decorating, at attending events. She has become a specialist in her field. ''It takes time, and I have to say that it would have been impossible to do the volunteer work I've done if my family had not been behind me, saying 'Go ahead. Your contributions are important.' Ted and the girls, from the time they were little, have always seemed proud of me—that is, as long as I keep my sense of humor and don't take myself too seriously. Ted has always felt that it was great that I had the opportunity to do things to help our city when I could," she says, as she begins to smile. "He did finally ask me to have the calls stop at home by early evening, so we would quit work at the same time."

Annette Strauss has worked in capacities other than fund raising, but it is as a fund raiser that she has become legend. When planning a benefit, she watches the expense column with her eye toward profit margins as carefully as any good corporate officer. "The purpose is to raise money for an important cause, and most of those who attend don't expect or want too much extravagance. And in the final analysis, Dallas' Department of Consumer Affairs sets the standards for fund-raising events with regulations which necessitate keeping costs at a minimum. Of course, it's very important that everyone have a good time, to feel that they had a memorable evening for the money they gave. But you know, you don't have to serve caviar. There are some who will do this because their husbands want their event to be very special and they are willing to pay for it personally. Given the choices, I'd rather my husband give the caviar money to the organization we're benefitting."

Annette Strauss is up early, and when she is not at her office, her telephone begins ringing by eight in the morning. Notes are made in a detailed datebook, index cards are filled, chores are assigned or received as she sits on the kingsize bed at the center of a broad circle of paperwork.

It becomes quickly obvious why doors open for Annette Strauss. Even while talking about her own work, she solicits information, with an attitude of genuine concern, about the work, opinions and families of those who question her. She lauds her two daughters, Nancy and Janie, both Phi Beta Kappa graduates of UT Austin and each named the outstanding woman student on campus, but she never forgets to ask about your children. She talks of her hectic schedule, but always asks about your day. She is achievement oriented but not driven, optimistic but not saccharin. She is an attractive woman with deep dimples echoing her ready smiles and dark hair always smoothly in place; but she is usually first with a compliment, quickly admiring a pretty blouse or handsome tie worn by those with whom she is conversing.

"I never ask people to give until it hurts; I ask them to give until they feel good. And, you know, there are always a few who are basically stingy and selfish who won't do or give anything unless it's for themselves. So I've learned not to waste my time with them. They're missing a lot in life, I think."

Most of the business leaders of the Dallas community have come to know Annette Strauss by her first name. She has knocked at their doors often in the past. But when she enters their homes or offices she doesn't worry that they might think she has come asking for money once again. "They know I am. But I don't care and neither do they. I'm not asking for myself. And we laugh about it. I do try not to take much of their time, so I only talk about what's really important. For example, . . . there are certain points I try to emphasize, like the basic importance of the performing arts to their own particular business. They all know that the arts are a tremendous economic asset; they just often need to be reminded. So often, Dallas' cultural resources are cited as a primary reason why quality business executives and professional talent choose to locate in Dallas—and STAY here. Before a large corporation moves its base of operations, after asking about the supply of workers, taxes and schools, it asks, 'Is the cultural situation right? What have you got to offer my employees, their families, their children? Are they going to have a well-rounded life?' It's very important, and I make certain to get that point across."

Annette Strauss does not hesitate to credit improvements throughout Texas to the work of women volunteers, mentioning child care centers, creative learning schools and educational opportunity programs created by women in Dallas as examples. "Texas, and our society, is changing rapidly, and women have become an increasingly vital and effective force in guiding the quality of our development. But what appears especially distinctive about the work of women in Texas is that it is anything but a gentle diversion. I like to believe that we work not for our own special interests, but for the general good. We are partners in the pursuits of our husbands, and we are capable of making tangible contributions to our communities. That is probably a characteristic of our heritage.

"Today, it is a fact that the quantitative growth of our state and the progress of our economies owes a substantial debt to the quality of the work performed by women in our civic, charitable and community affairs. The very fact that more and more women recognize the opportunities, sense the excitement and expend the effort makes me extremely confident that we're just beginning to have an impact. Texas women, I feel, are vastly more interested in where they plan to go in the future than in congratulating themselves on how far they've come."

Sally Walsh

Lean, sleek, uncluttered, classic—adjectives often used to describe the interior spaces that Sally Walsh has programmed, designed and furnished—double as descriptions of her own appearance and spirit. Since arriving in Houston in 1955, Walsh has pioneered the use of bold-colored, crisp-lined contemporary furnishings and office space, leaving an unmistakable mark on hundreds of banks and university buildings, executive offices and hospitals, oil company headquarters and even a few Lear jets. Her work has been recognized by the American Institute of Architects, the American Society of Interior Designers and other design organizations. But, asked to discuss her accolades, she shrugs and responds, "My dear, I'm terribly unimpressed with awards. It is nice, don't get me wrong, to be honored by your peers. And I'm particularly touched when they do because I don't belong to anything. But I don't place much value in awards in general, and I tend to forget the details."

Walsh's private studio is a Whistler-like study in black and white, tucked high above the noise of the street in the tower of a downtown Houston office building. It is here that she would come, for a few hours or a long Saturday, from her office at S. I. Morris Associates, to work on designs for textiles and furniture, following up on ideas that race through her mind during spare moments. That her "get-away" spot was actually a second office is a clue to Walsh's dedication to her work. "I'm convinced that attitude is the determining factor for success in a field. Success requires total dedication to superior performance coupled with a judicious narrowing of the scope of one's field of expertise . . . . The more normal one's personal life is, particularly in the case of a woman, the broader the proliferation of her energy, with the resulting lessening of her chances of ultimate recognition as an expert in any one area,'' Walsh says.

In a deep and throaty voice, she recalls her father, a mining engineer who read Plato for pleasure, recited Gertrude Stein outloud while laughing delightedly, and played complex games based on pure mathematics. After her father died when she was ten, her mother took Walsh and her older sister to live with family in Sioux Falls, South Dakota. She was enrolled in a disciplined girls' school where she learned to ''conjugate 101 irregular French verbs,'' confided in her mathematics teacher that ''all numbers were colors,'' and discovered that ''Shakespeare was the fourth God.''

But living in her grandparents' home was a chaotic nightmare. ''My grandfather was in the throes of senile dementia, ranting from dawn to dark,'' she remembers. ''And my uncle, who lived there also, hated everyone when he was drunk, and he was that by four-thirty every day of his life. My sister and I would run home from school, go immediately to our rooms, and lock the door, and stay there until my mother came home from her job. It was a hard and difficult life.''

While still living at home, Walsh attended a small college for one and one-half years. This experience led finally to ''rebellious boredom'' and a desperate desire to get away. Within two months of arriving in Chicago, Walsh was into and out of nearly a dozen jobs. ''I had learned to put up with anything at home, but outside my home . . . I don't like to be uncomfortable. So, whenever an employer or work conditions made me uncomfortable, I got my purse and left.''

She finally landed a job with ''no complications and nice people'' and might have stayed there forever, she says. But friends, who knew she was interested in pursuing a career in design, encouraged her to interview for a job with Hans Knoll, who had come to Chicago to open his first showroom outside of New York. ''I guess I got the job because Hans was impressed that I had heard of and knew about the work of everyone whose furniture designs Hans had included in his catalogue. I had my mother to thank for that. She was tremendously interested in art and architecture [Her mother would exclaim, 'Chagall? NO, no. Can't you see—it's Miro!'] . . . She made certain that we had plenty of books and periodicals, and

178

that we read them and kept abreast of what was developing in the arts. She was stuck with two young daughters for companionship, and she brought us up to her level of conversation rather than just talking about what we did at school.

"At any rate, I knew about the new designers, and that impressed [Knoll]. He also knew that, except for a little experience working for an interior designer . . . , I was untrained, so that he wouldn't have to unlearn any traditional ideas I had concerning design. It was a wonderful time to be with Knoll, only a short distance from the embryo stage of his firm. I was hired to do everything: type, write orders, call on clients, sell in the showroom, walk the sheepdog—everything involved with keeping the business running . . . . I had the whole range of experience."

Her work included flying to the Philippines to check on teak shipments, tours to the West Coast to seek additional showroom space and an occasional celebrity customer as well. Marlene Dietrich once called the Knoll showroom in Chicago, upon learning that she was to become a grandmother, and asked for an Eero Saarinen womb chair for her children's home. Anticipating babysitting chores, Dietrich also wanted an ottoman for the chair so that she could put her feet up as she crooned lullabies to her grandchild. "Up until then Saarinen had refused to do ottomans, and we told her that," Walsh recalls. "She called him up, and made the request herself. Now the Saarinen ottoman is part of the permanent collection."

Walsh eventually became the head of the Chicago showroom, responsible for a five-state area. But shortly after she married, her husband took a job in Houston, and she left Knoll. After working briefly for a major furnishings and design store, she and a partner opened their own small design firm. "I guess some of the things that we did then were pretty far out for that time in Houston, although they wouldn't have been for New York or Paris. People here weren't used to good contemporary design . . . and I was NOT going to give them anything else," she chuckles. "My mother always insisted that my sister and I be polite, so I always am. But I do dig my heels in on very important matters of design."

One project brought her fledgling firm publicity that she can laugh about now. Hired to plan and design a student center at Rice University, Walsh and her partner chose brilliant orange Herman Miller desks and bright blue Eames chairs. But the budget was trimmed just before completion of the project, so the blue covers were left off the chairs in favor of plain white. Rice was left with an alumni office furnished in the signature colors of the University of Texas; Walsh and her partner, a graduate of the UT School of Architecture, were left red-faced.

Walsh did not then and still does not like to work on residential projects. So, when she and her partner disagreed over handling residential designs, the partnership was amicably ended. Walsh worked for a while with another commercial firm and was a consultant for most of the major design firms in the Houston area. In 1972, she joined S. I. Morris Associates. As the only woman partner in a firm of about two dozen architects and planners, Walsh coordinated the interior architectural design for many massive projects, including the Houston Central Public Library (300,000 square feet), Braniff International headquarters in Dallas (400,000 square feet) and the Gulf Oil Company headquarters in Houston (400,000 square feet).

Beginning with the gutted space inside a building, Walsh programs the needs of her clients, planning the location of all interior walls and doors, type and placement of lighting, electrical equipment, even outlets, before she selects the colors and finish of walls and floors and chooses furnishings. She may even accompany a client to other cities choosing art for the building.

''What I am really interested in is the working person's environment, where employees spend every daylight hour . . . . That continues to be fascinating just because it changes constantly with the economic situation. Today, you pay so much for a square foot of space in a building that you absolutely cannot just hand out grandiose space to people any longer . . . . Now [you have] to crush ever more people into space without their knowing it, without their realizing that they've lost space,'' she says. ''And if recession comes, instead of planning space in brand new structures, I would start using space in existing structures to house people more efficiently.''

Many of her clients are banks, and the contemporary space she creates fits ''like a glove for the new approach in banking. The attitude now is to project an image of 'Come on in pal; we're your friend.' That's a complete reversal of the image of the grand old man sitting behind a carved mahogany desk and being austere. And if they want traditional banks, they go to someone else. I simply don't take on projects of a traditional nature.''

Walsh takes special pride in the appearance of the Houston Central Public Library. ''People going to a public library should see good design. That may be their only exposure to it.'' She defines good interior architectural design as ''one which meets and improves upon the working needs of the individuals housed, does so within the budget, then transcends these vital practical considerations to create an imaginative pleasure-giving environment.'' Walsh says that in ''public buildings, it is particularly important to strive for perfection in the creative use and modulation of space . . . . Each piece of furniture—indeed every object in the building—should be of classic good design, manufactured with impeccable adherance to the original design.''

Throughout the Central Library are original Mies van der Rohe Barcelona chairs and tables, Sebastian Matta foam blocks and Marcel Bruer Cesca chairs. The only objects in the Central Library which do not meet ''classic'' good design criteria, Walsh says, are those such as display cases and carrels that she designed to meet specific needs. ''And I must admit, I failed to exercise selection control over the cleaning equipment—an oversight I regret!''

During a lazy Christmas Day in 1979, strolling in the chill but clear air of South Dakota, Walsh thought deeply about what she still wanted to accomplish. ''I came to the conclusion that to honor my priorities, I must leave the firm . . . . Now I am in the Gulf Building office daily, with the intention of spending the next few years in product design—furniture, textiles, a jacket and purse for working women—and in writing a book,'' she says. There are no plans to form a company. After nearly thirty years of working with a company, she says, ''I am enjoying the reality of being an individual again.''

Walsh is constantly thinking of new and better design plans. Her vacations are usually taken in major metropolian areas where, rather than rest, she seeks out new buildings to examine and analyze. ''I have a prodigious amount of energy,'' she says, ''and it's a major problem for me. I can't turn my brain off.'' The last time she tried a restful vacation, spending a weekend at a lake resort near Houston, she recalls, ''My brain was churning madly and I thought, I have to do something, but I'm not going to work on any projects. So instead, I designed a line of textiles that I will probably market. Doing that was such a relief for me, more relaxing than lying in the sun with a book.''

Sarah Weddington

As Sarah Weddington rises from her place of honor at the speaker's dias and begins to address a gathering of attentive Democrats assembled in Dallas, it is the work of a pro: a smattering of Texas jokes; statistics to support a recent decision of the Carter Administraton; sufficient discussion of women's issues to keep women in the audience leaning forward, but not so much that the men begin to grow restless in their metal folding chairs; remembrances of law school to reinforce her common bonds with the attorneys in the crowd; a little talk of pending legislation; a few more Texas tales. She returns to her chair with a modest smile as the audience rises to an enthusiastic ovation.

Months later, in Texas for a seminar at the University of Houston, she has two hours before her speech will be given, but there is no last minute rush to study notes, no nervous walk around the room to calm nerves. She settles herself, shoes off, onto the sofa in the university hotel suite, and concentrates on yet another interview. She has the confident, but not cocky, attitude of one who knows not only her subject, but herself.

Her appearance is deceiving. Stawberry blonde hair twisted up in a neat schoolmarm's roll, ultrasuede suits and bow-at-the-neck blouses, a string of pearls and comfortable pumps—all combine to present the image of a genteel Southern lady, more comfortable in the audience than before the speaker's lectern. Critics describe Sarah Ragle Weddington as velvet-gloved, perhaps too soft-spoken to be effective.

Despite this low-key style or, more likely, because of it, Weddington has been, in quick succession, a successful lawyer who argued one of the most controversial cases of the 1970's before the Supreme Court, a three-term state legislator, general counsel for the U. S. Department of Agriculture in charge of more than two hundred lawyers, and an assistant to the President.

Weddington was born in Abilene in 1945, the first child of a Methodist minister and his wife. Church assignments took the family to Canyon and later to Vernon, but they returned to Abilene where Weddington graduated, a member of the basketball team but not a class officer, at age sixteen. Three years later she graduated with honors from McMurry College. Frustrated with student teaching and realizing that she would have to spend many years in graduate school before she could teach at the college level, Weddington decided to attend the University of Texas Law School.

In 1970, after starting a law practice in Austin, Weddington joined forces with another young attorney, Linda Coffee of Dallas, to challenge Texas law prohibiting abortions. A federal district court in Dallas agreed with the two that the U. S. Constitution protected the fundamental right of a woman to choose whether to have children and that the Texas law should be thrown out. That decision, which was appealed by the state, put Weddington on the path toward the Supreme Court. She spent two months researching her case, preparing a 165-page brief, 17-page supplementary (filed for reargument) and nearly 500 pages of legal, medical and sociological data to support the case. Weddington argued the case before seven Supreme Court justices in December, 1971; six months later the Court asked for reargument so that the two newly appointed justices could take part in the decision. The 7-2 decision throwing out the Texas law came nearly three years after the first case was filed and after Sarah Weddington had already moved on to the Texas legislature.

Her decision to run for the state house resulted from Weddington's efforts to interest Texas legislators in women's issues. ''I had lobbied a lot in the legislature in 1971, and I was distressed that they didn't want to handle women's issues. In 1972 we were beginning to form the National Women's Political Caucus, and some of us were helping form the Texas caucus. We were sitting around, about nine of us, and talking, and said in essence that the only way to get women's issues dealt with is for women to run for the legislature, and to run their own campaigns. So two days before the filing deadline, I went down and withdrew the money and filed for office.

''I had not done any of the things I would say to anybody else to do now. I hadn't checked with anybody. I didn't have any funds built up. I wasn't particularly known in the community. But it was a combination of lucky factors. The favored candidate in the race didn't run at the last minute. The incumbent was running for another office. The opponents I had weren't as good as I was. It was right after the Sharpstown scandals in Texas, and people were willing to think about having new people who looked different from the old image which you usually think of as a legislator. So it was a combination of events.''

Weddington spent three terms in the legislature where friendships with Lt. Governor Bill Hobby and then house parliamentarian Bob Johnson helped hone her political skills. ''I studied politics as a process, and it's a process that has two aspects: one is substance and one is people, and you cannot ignore either one and be totally successful. So that I really did work very hard at knowing the substance well, but the people aspect of it was also important, and that did not come naturally to me.

''I read an article recently that said that women in mid-level management in government emphasize so much hard work, diligence, doing a good job, that sometimes they overlook the personal aspects necessary to make it to top-level positions. And it's a lesson I have learned. Really, who you know, and how you contact them, and how you work with them is very important, particularly in the legislature. That is a group where, a lot of times, people vote for or against things based on who's supporting them. I was always honest with people about my feelings on issues and who I was as a person, but I made it a point of finding things about all the members that I could respect and like and enjoy. There were very few of the members that I would not consider my friends.''

Even as she acknowledges that she has enjoyed socializing in Washington, D.C., meeting people she has read about, and having the White House gates swing open to admit her small car—all perquisites for a Presidential advisor—she is quick to add that nothing was ever more fun than country western dancing at the Broken Spoke in Austin with friends from the legislature. ''Every Tuesday night everybody went to the Broken Spoke, and all the members were my friends, and it meant I had eighty dancing partners. I got to dance every dance and it was wonderful. If I had to choose between a Washington cocktail party and dancing the Cotton-eyed Joe at the Broken Spoke, there is no question about what I would do,'' she says, laughing when it is pointed out that, as is politically wise, she has intimated an answer without stating one. ''The Broken Spoke, of course!'' she says.

Her sentiments for her home state run deep. Vacations are often spent canoeing and horseback riding with a friend's family in Telegraph. ''That's about forty miles outside of Junction,'' she explains, obviously certain that she has thus pinpointed it. Her parents live now in Lubbock, and Weddington visits them as often as her schedule permits. Her voting address remains in Austin, where she leased rather than sold her home when she went to Washington.

Weddington says she took the position of general counsel for the Department of Agriculture in 1977 because she wanted to work in a field that would expand her knowledge and influence beyond women's affairs, but one that would also be relevant and beneficial to Texans. She resigned that position in late 1978 to accept the position of presidential advisor without designation (which meant she was not limited to women's issues although her efforts were concentrated on them) and moved into the basement office at the White House left vacant by Midge Constanza. In late 1979 Weddington became a member of the White House senior staff. As assistant to the President with a staff of thirty-five people answering to her, Weddington served a combined role handling women's issues and acting as the White House liaison to the state Democratic parties and the Carter-Mondale reelection campaign. The new job gave Weddington a broader, more political role, including arranging briefing sessions on domestic and foreign policy, but the women's issues were not dropped from her area of interest. ''When I got my new office, everyone said that women's issues had moved out of the basement and up to the top floor,'' she says.

When she first became a presidential advisor, Weddington set several goals for herself. ''Certainly one part of it would be to become one of the most trusted and respected members of the White House staff . . . . The second . . . would be to help change public opinion about women. And third would be change in specific issues. Helping to pass the ERA would be one. The appointment of more women is very significant to me. I think the more women you appoint, the more role models you have, the more women you have who are in a position to change policies. More women can hire other women.

''In terms of the theme of the administration, the one I have chosen for women is that we as an administration offer choices. We're for women having the choice of being wife and mother, to be honored, respected and not penalized for it; to have the option of combining family and work outside the home; or the option of placing emphasis on the professional. I spent a lot of time developing those, because I think there hasn't been that sense of unity among women, saying that there are various choices and that we support the right of any woman to make any of those choices and to change from time to time.''

Part of the difficulties in securing passage of the Equal Rights Amendment, Weddington says, is due to the fear many women have of what will be expected of them. ''ERA has almost come to represent change in our lives. And I think there are many women who have grown up in the mode of people telling you what was expected. You live that role and everything was supposed to be all right. And suddenly, we're saying, 'It's not that easy. You make choices for yourself and your personal roles and you have to rely on yourself a lot.' ''

Weddington says it is hard for women in Texas to feel personally affected by ratification of the ERA because of recent changes in state laws that ''by and large make women legally equal in Texas. So other than on principal . . . and on making it a national issue and extending the same protection to other women, it's hard for women in Texas to feel personally affected by ERA.

''My theory is that Texas is something of a unique state. It's a state that is not part of the Old South in the sense that there are very few old families here . . . we are not bound by the old traditions, even as pertains to women, that the Old South might be, for example. Women here helped settle the prairies. And it's also a state where you have so many new people coming in and the state is developing so rapidly, that you look for people and talent where you can find it. The state has never had a stereotyped role for women as other places and the pioneer tradition has allowed women to be stronger.''

There are many people who believe that Texas may soon be ready to elect a woman to statewide office. That woman most likely will be someone very similar to Sarah Weddington—someone who can talk about ''contacts'' without making the word seem profane; who has worked for women's rights but has not excluded other important issues from her efforts; whose Texas identity is so strong that it can endure exposure to Potomac Fever; who can discuss points of law with influential urban legal groups, and also sit on the back of a pickup truck talking price supports and subsidies with farmers. Someone who, in that strong network of ''good ole boys,'' can be accepted as a ''good ole Texas girl.''

Mary West

Her chauffeur drove her through the front gate, around the "no parking" signs and past policemen who shook their heads "no" in vain, right up to the front entrance of Freeman Coliseum in San Antonio. Mary West was going to the Fat Stock Show and Rodeo, and she wasn't about to wait in line. Before going down to her box seats near the arena, she settles upstairs at a table in the Frontier Room, orders "the best vodka you have, straight," and holds court. Rodeo officials and box-seat holders, walking to tables laden with fried chicken and sizzling steaks, pause to pay her homage with a tip of the hat or a handshake. Later, as she walks through the livestock barns, West stops to inspect a horse owned by a friend, asking "What's this horse broke for?"

"Why, Mary, I guess Twister is broke to do anything but the dishes," comes the answer, and she joins the laughter. Mary West is in town for rodeo, but also for business.

She was born in San Antonio in her grandparents' home on King William Street. But if you ask her when that was, or anything else she does not feel like divulging, she is liable to turn away and talk at length with someone else before forgiving your transgression and again acknowledging your presence. One thing she does enjoy talking about in detail is her Texas heritage. Her grandfather West made fourteen trips across the Chisolm Trail leading into the state when Texas was still frontier country. Her maternal grandfather, Alfred Thomas Bedell, was chosen Texas' first adjutant general soon after the Texas militia was formed. Mary West was raised, the younger of two daughters, on the Rafter R, the family ranch near Batesville, now run by her daughter, Mary Nan West. Her father, George West, was a well-known Texas rancher, who had a town named after him; her mother was "president and chairman of everything in Batesville."

Mary West grew up wanting to do two things, ranch and be a lawyer. "My father could do the work of three men and I was the only person who could ever work along by his side. I could take it. When I was a little girl, I had my own punching bag . . . . I was riding horses when I was two years old, and by the time I was five, my daddy was teaching me to shoot . . . . I knew I wanted to be a rancher. And my mother's brother was a lawyer and I greatly admired him. So I wanted to be a lawyer too."

When she was ready for college, West attended the University of California at Berkeley and Cumberland Law School in Tennessee. At her parents' urging she returned to Texas to start a law practice, about the time "Sarah Hughes was going full steam in Dallas," she recalls. "Was she ever good looking . . . very bright. But there weren't too many of us women practicing law then. I never intended to practice law but ten years. We had no legal aid society at that time, and I said I'd give ten years of my life to help people who were poor. I had a few clients that weren't poor, because you have to pay the bills, but ninety percent of them were poor."

She was married for a few years to a fellow Texan, but that marriage ended in divorce when her daughter was four years old. "We never discuss it," she says firmly. "I had my name and my daughter's name changed back to West. I've always agreed with women keeping their maiden names, and I've always fought for it. So did my father, because you see, he had no sons and he liked the idea of having his name carried on. As a matter of fact, the West men were very progressive. They believed in women having equal rights and they believed that if a woman had property, it belonged to her and no one should come in and take charge of it."

After giving up her law practice, West purchased her first ranch, the 3C, four thousand acres near Oracle, Arizona. "I found Arizona to be a much more progressive state than any part of Texas at that time, although South Texas was becoming a bit more progressive. When my father came out and saw the type of set-up I had on my corrals, he immediately decided to rebuild his . . . . We swapped ideas; I learned from him and he didn't mind learning from me."

West purchased her current cattle operation, the Spike S, near El Paso in 1969. The cattle brand bears a marked resemblance to a dollar sign. "I own more beefalo than anyone else, several thousand of them . . . . Oh, honey, I can just sell them like hotcakes. I'm selling them for meat. They mature very quickly, and the meat is very delicious. It's low in cholesterol and very tasty," she exclaims.

"I have what we call half bloods, that's a first cross of Charolais and buffalo. I have the second cross coming on, which are three-quarters buffalo . . . . I will determine within the next two or three years what the breaking point is from a monetary standpoint, how far away we should go from pureblood, and I'll chop it off there."

In addition to the beefalo, West has registered herds of Hereford and Charolais and commercial herds of both. And when she is short-handed on the ranch, she helps with the roundup. "I had a bunch of bulls for sale not long ago. Well, one cowboy got sick and another didn't show up. So I only had one cowboy. I got in my Suburban and I said he could use my horse at the corral. I told him I'd round up 75 percent of the bulls and he could go pick up the girls . . . . There's not any difference in using a Suburban than in using a horse to round up if you know what you're doing." But unlike family members at other ranches, West refuses to use helicopters for her roundups.

During hunting season, she takes off from the paved roads that cross the Spike S and, with her apricot poodle, Tango, beside her, shoots her limit of dove and quail from the Suburban. "I probably have the only poodle in Texas that will retrieve game birds," she says proudly.

Against advice, West planted apple and pecan trees on the Spike S. Now those who advised against the venture can stop along the road to purchase fruit and nuts from the flourishing pecan groves and apple orchards on the ranch. And if West is nearby, she'll not forget to reminisce about the poor advice.

Her Little Spike ranch, located outside of Tucson, is a 30-acre spread with "a rather attractive hacienda," West says. Here she raises squab, pigeons, guineas, and "turkeys that cost so much to raise they should be gold-plated." While there are no oil rigs on the two ranches she owns outright, West receives substantial royalties from the West Ranch Hills, located in Jackson County, Texas, as part of an inheritance.

Mary West says she never found that being a woman was a disadvantage in her ranching career. "You must remember that my name was WEST. There were a lot of West men living. So anyone in the ranching business would naturally have some respect for the men of my family. And after all, there wasn't a cowboy in the state that could outride me and there were few Texas Rangers that could out-shoot me. So what was the disadvantage?"

Mary West died at her ranch in Hudspeth County on April 16, 1980, during the preparation of this book.

Edna Gardner Whyte

When she made her first licensing check flight in a tiny OX-5 Swallow, her examiner remained on the ground, directing her with hand signals from the safety of the runway: He wasn't about to fly with a woman. It was 1926 and for nearly a year Edna Gardner Whyte had been squeezing $35 a week from her $70 salary as a registered nurse in Seattle to pay for flying lessons. "One of my patients had taken me up for a ride and I knew when I stepped back onto the ground after that first flight that flying was what I wanted to do. Lots of people thought that aviation was a lark, a passing fad, that the bi-plane was too clumsy. I had a lot of faith in the growth of aviation."

Her mother stopped sending money for Whyte's schooling when she learned that her headstrong daughter was continuing, against parental prohibitions, with flying lessons. But Whyte, refusing to give up her passion for planes, eventually overcame the protests of her mother and even taught her to fly. Years later, when her mother was eighty-five, the two entered and won the Sky Lady Derby in Kansas City. "We entered three races that year. Mother got more press than I did."

While still a young nurse, Whyte moved to New Bedford, Massachusetts, joined the Navy Nurse Corps and became known in headlines as "The Flying Nurse" as she won competitions in cross-country racing, aerobatic contests and even bomb-dropping events. When *Look* magazine in 1938 featured the top female pilots in the world, women with the most flying time, Edna Gardner was among them. "You ask anybody in high school now and all they know is Jacqueline Cochran and Amelia Earhart. Earhart never instructed, never flew in competition, never was in any races. Neither Earhart nor Cochran had enough hours to make that *Look* group, but they both had enough money to hire a promoter who could put them in the headlines," Whyte says.

After she left the service, Whyte moved to New Orleans and opened a flight instruction school on her own ground, with her own hangers, shop and offices. "Many of my students were women. One came in furious because her husband was taking lessons on the sly. While I was calming her down, she heard a pretty, young girl talking about her first cross-country flight. When the woman found out she could take lessons too, she was thrilled and she went on to become one of my best students."

In 1941, when the Navy built a large base in New Orleans and took over all available airports, Whyte sold her New Orleans Air College and moved to Ft. Worth. "I had always dreamed of living in Texas. When I was a little girl in grade school, I thought of Texas as a large, wide open space, a wonderful place to live. I had heard that they had had a woman governor, and I thought that any state that would vote for a woman governor would be a place of fair-minded people."

In the early stages of World War II, Whyte was hired to teach instrument flying to many Army and Navy pilots. "In February 1944, General Arnold said he had enough pilots trained, so the government discontinued the war training pilots' program. Since I had been a Navy nurse for six and a half years, I put in for my Army nurse commission, and I served, attached to the famous 249th Unit Hospital, near Clark Field at Lusen in the Philippines." While there she would occasionally test damaged planes.

After returning to Ft. Worth, she married fellow pilot and instructor George M. Whyte, and together they operated Aero Enterprise at Meachum Field in Ft. Worth from 1953 until 1973 when her husband died. "There were marriage proposals earlier in my life, but everytime they came, I looked at the man and looked at my airplanes and I chose airplanes. With George, I didn't have to make a choice." Although she never had children of her own, she continues to have a close relationship with her husband's daughter from his previous marriage.

Whyte decided in 1970 that she wanted her own airstrip and found the perfect spot in Roanoke, eighty-five acres of flat land about twenty miles northeast of Ft. Worth. "I came out here hoping to just have a hangar to keep my three planes in, and the first thing I knew, there were twenty-three airplanes on top of me wanting hangar space, just for a chance to use an old mud strip. I finally had to build hangars for them and put in a good runway for the better and bigger airplanes, and the airport just grew.'' Now her Aero Valley Airport has hangar space for 124 airplanes. Sometimes, as when neighbor Bunker Hunt hosts a large Charolais auction that attracts cattlemen from across the West, who fly into Roanoke in their own planes, she could use more space.

The airport, with its flying school, restaurant, maintenance services and hangars, is not only a place of business for Whyte but also home. Behind the office, whose walls are lined with newspaper clippings about the ''Flying Nurse'' and with trophy cases jam-packed with prizes and gilded airplanes atop loving cups, there are a few rooms where Edna Whyte lives. Pilots who need her airport and students who need her counsel never have to look far to find her.

Since beginning her operation in Roanoke, Whyte has soloed almost seven hundred student pilots. ''I enjoy molding an individual into a good, safe pilot. To me, that's the challenge I take on. I have to change his or her thinking, reactions, habits, and teach judgment and safety.'' Many of the younger students are the children of men and women whom Whyte and her late husband taught at Meachum Field. Several stewardesses based in the Dallas-Ft. Worth area take flying instructions regularly, and some have been hired to pilot aircraft for corporations in the state. Others are preparing for jobs with the larger airline companies.

If Texans had run the airlines earlier in the century, Whyte might have talked her way into the cockpit of commercial passenger planes. ''During the war I was a flight instrument instructor with many men instructors, and I was accepted as an equal. The men students often asked for me. My experience has been that Texas accepts a woman in a man's job.

''I tried to get a job as a commercial pilot with several of the big companies in the late thirties. They all turned me down because I was a woman. I had fifteen airplanes of my own and had hours and hours of flight time. Some of the men I taught were given jobs. One airline said I was too short. I stood by one of my students who they hired and I was a good two inches taller than he was!''

Some of her male friends who had airline jobs are now retired, drawing several thousand dollars a month in pensions, while Whyte continues to work almost nine hours a day, seven days a week. ''One of them told me he would trade his pension and his beach chair in Florida for the chance to own and operate my school. I told him that with my luck, he'd drop dead and I'd be left with nothing,'' she laughed.

Although she jokes about her bad luck, she has had her share of the good kind. During the thirties, when she was the only registered nurse in the United States with a pilot's transport license, she was asked to copilot a flight from New York to Rome and to conduct tests for pilot fatigue and stress. At the last minute Whyte was ordered back to duty and another nurse was sent in her place. The plane went down over the Azores, and all aboard were killed. "That's made me a fatalist. What's going to be is going to be," Whyte says. Her only crash landing came in 1933 when she ran out of gas while circling Long Island as she waited for the fog to lift. Her plane suffered $500 worth of damage, but Whyte was unhurt. "I had crashed into the Woolworth Estate on Oyster Bay. It was probably the only way to get in there uninvited!" Whyte had just won a Kate Smith trophy race at New York's Roosevelt Field, and the five-hundred-dollar prize went to repair her plane for the next competition.

Her luck, however, held in competitions: Whyte has won the Powder Puff Derby six times and has taken four first-place ribbons in the more treacherous International Angel Derby, which she has entered twenty-two times. More than a hundred trophies overflow the glass case in the corner of her office, prizes from air races and contests throughout the United States, Canada and Central America.

In the early sixties, Whyte bought an Air Commander 200 and with seven other female pilots flew air races in the International Air Race competitions in Texas, Nevada, Florida, Indiana and Washington. "We flew our planes 25 feet off the ground at 200 miles an hour, and we never scratched an airplane or a girl. We were getting around $9,000 for each air show and we'd take that money and pay each girl's expenses to the show and home again. Then we'd take the rest and divide it up between the three top winners. The men couldn't stand it, us winning all that money. So they bought Army surplus planes and went to the race committee, which was all men, and asked them to take us off the program and give them that money and spot. The race committee did it. And many people in the grandstands have come to me and said, 'I'm interested in buying a stock model for my personal use and you girls were flying those. I could see which one performed the best. I'll never buy one of those old surplus planes.'"

Whyte still flies in several races a year and has plans to continue flying as long as she passes her physical examination. "I want to fly 'til I'm at least 100," she says, "and that's less than a quarter of a century away."

In her career spanning more than fifty years, Whyte has completed twenty-six flight log books and comes closer daily to filling her twenty-seventh as she flies one of her four planes into the skies over Roanoke.

She has flown more than 25,000 hours and taught more than 3,000 students. Whyte was inducted into the Aviation Hall of Fame by the OX-5 Club of America in 1975. She has served as president of the 99 Club, the international organization of licensed women pilots. In more than half a century of flying, Whyte has been away from her planes only once when she returned to her nursing career for a year and a half during the polio epidemic of 1949–1950.

Whyte is pleased that qualified women are holding an increasing number of ''good positions'' with the airlines and is proud that, from her barnstorming days in New England to her years of teaching in Texas, she has helped open the skies for women pilots. ''All I ever wanted to do was to prove that women could do it, that they could do a good job in aviation. I guess I was just born forty years before my time.''

Irene Wischer

The office is fitting for an oil executive: Geological maps framed in rich woods dominate the walls, oil rigs in brass and silver dot the tops of the large desk and sideboard, and several golf trophies emerge from under the folders and petroleum publications. Behind the desk the company president, telephone to ear, is negotiating a new lease contract with a voice that is at once friendly, confident and firm. Conversation over, she replaces her earring, folds her arms across the desk and flashes a let's-get-down-to-business smile.

Although Irene Wischer is not the only woman in the traditionally male-dominated oil and gas industry, she is one of the few who has worked her way from the typewriter to the top. As she talks about her career, she speaks with pride but never vanity. She is usually a reserved woman, but not always. She can crack jokes with the best of the rig workers or complain forcefully and knowledgeably about government regulation of her industry. Yet her toughness is tempered with a solicitous quality: Wischer can call you ''honey'' and not be patronizing, offer advice and not be pedantic.

When talking business, Wischer is animated, her face and features expressive. But when conversation turns to her family life, husband and two grown step-children, she is cooly reticent. ''My husband has no part in my career, none whatsoever,'' she says, later adding that she prefers to remain a ''low-key'' person, and but for the encouragement that her example might give young people, she avoids publicity.

Born in Nebraska, she moved to Texas as a child after her father ''went broke'' during the 1930's. She had planned a career in teaching, but for economic reasons, she was forced to go to work to support herself. She took a secretarial job with a small oil company owned by Frank Henderson in San Antonio and set about learning the responsibilities both of her own job and that of others. "I really cut my teeth on gasoline," she says, recalling a time when the company in which she is now a stockholder was primarily involved with gasoline recycling and repressuring plants. "I joined the company when residue was in short demand, selling for about four cents. Now it is selling for more than two dollars."

When Henderson died in 1943, a trust was established that was responsible for the company. Because the trustees lived out of state, they depended on Wischer and her knowledge of the firm to keep things running smoothly. Following the purchase of the company by new owners, Wischer became a director of the firm in 1950. Within two years, she was named president. What began as the Henderson Company has developed into diversified interests: Henderson Properties, North Star Petroleum Corporation, Panhandle Producing Company, Paladin Pipeline Company, and Pinto Well Servicing Company. The companies Irene Wischer now heads have more than 200 oil wells, over 100 gas wells, a gathering system, well service equipment and leases across the state. Until 1973, all of the drilling that Wischer undertook was "straight up," totally owned by her firm, but now her company co-ventures some leases, never taking less than a one-quarter interest.

When she took her secretarial job in the early 1940's, Wischer had no secret schemes to advance to the top. "At the time it would have been ridiculous even if I had thought of it," she says. But in a rare moment of self-reflection, she notes, "I've always been eager, competitive, ambitious. I've always liked competition; it makes me work harder. And I like responsibility . . . VERY MUCH. I worked hard, and I didn't pay any attention to hours and I tried to learn as much as I could about the industry.

"It was also circumstances, opportunity, a matter of being in the right place at the right time. I had some peers and mentors who liked me, who had confidence in my keeping them informed. If I had to sum up a requirement for getting to the top of any company, given ability and hard work, it would be through good communication. I had learned a lot about the industry and about this particular company, and I was in a position where people had to rely on me for my knowledge and my ability to communicate that knowledge."

She pauses only a moment before adding, "I also feel that someone has to take an interest in your career. With men as well as women, unless you are one of those few who start at the top, if you are

200

going to work up through corporate levels past mid-management, someone will have to take an interest in you, recognize your ability, and reach down to help you."

Because much of her company's petroleum products are sold interstate, Wischer has developed an expertise in this aspect of the business. "I think if I have a forte, it is in the area of contract negotiations and federal regulations. I've spent a lot of time lobbying and testifying on behalf of independent producers like ourselves. You know, we have more federal agencies involved with our business, over seventy . . . ," and she begins rolling government names and acronyms off her tongue with an arched tone usually reserved for subcommittee meetings in Washington.

Wischer points to federal regulations as one of the major changes in her industry since she was hired as a secretary. "In 1954 the federal government began to regulate the interstate sale of gas at the well head, and the whole situation was changed. Prices were held artificially low, and that caused stacking of rigs and ceasing of drilling. There was a real, long period of recession in the industry . . . . Until the price at the gas pump went up, the collective public was never interested. The major companies had public information programs for decades, but the public never seemed to realize that the country was getting bigger in terms of demand and consumption."

But despite the increasing difficulties of doing business in the oil and gas industry, Wischer qualifies her grievances about the problems of the industry. "There is still a glamour to the business; there will always be because it is a gamble. You can improve your odds with knowledge, but it's still a gamble."

The words "first woman member" have appeared between two commas after Wischer's name for many years. She was the first businesswoman trustee at Southwest Research Institute, a nonprofit organization that focuses on applied research in engineering fields. She was the first woman elected to the board of directors of the National Bank of Commerce in San Antonio, the first to serve on the Business Advisory Council at St. Mary's University, the first to serve on the board of directors and as an officer of the San Antonio Chamber of Commerce, and the first woman officer of the Independent Petroleum Association of America. Frequently she accepted these positions, although they placed extra demands on her already busy schedule, because she felt the "doors needed to be opened for other women. As soon as one woman serves on board, it is easier for others to follow. These are the best times for women to move up in the business community," she says, but warns, "If we don't take advantage of our opportunities they will pass."

Wischer is surprised that so few women are involved in the oil and gas industry, particularly as wildcatters or independent oil operators. "There isn't anything to keep a woman from going out and drilling a well. There are certainly women who have the money. You can hire the knowledge, the production people, the geologists, the engineers. But women just haven't done it yet. Perhaps the risk factor does not appeal to them. Certainly, a woman would have to obtain financing to go out on her own. If she becomes an independent operator by advancing through the ranks while working for a company, she should certainly be qualified. I do not think that being a woman should be a hindrance. Her competency and willingness to work are more important to her success than her sex.

"However, if a woman is associated with a large oil company, statistics show that it has thus far been almost impossible to rise above mid-level management. It is at this level that moving ahead becomes exceedingly competitive, and women MAY not be as well accepted. This should change with more female lawyers, engineers and geologists entering the petroleum industry." The women who work for the companies Wischer heads are in clerical and secretarial positions. "We just haven't had many women apply for jobs as geologists or engineers. I think most of the young women are applying with the major companies instead."

Wischer has been a supporter of women's rights since long before the women's movement became as popular, or as unpopular, as it is today. "I'm not the type to go out and carry signs and enter a protest march, but I'm for ratification of the ERA. You will find most businesswomen are." As president of the Texas Federation of Republican Women and as a member of the national council on the status of women during both the Nixon and Ford administrations, she pushed for women's rights. But she recognizes that men's attitudes towards women have probably changed less in the oil and gas industry than in other industries.

Men who work for Wischer, however, have to get used to seeing a woman at the rig, even though they may still believe it is bad luck, for Wischer appears occasionally—in colorful but tailored dress, coordinated bracelets and earrings, and a hard hat—to inspect a site. "I HAVE to go to the rig from time to time. It gets me back to the business, to the most exciting part psychologically, to the place where the gamble is."

When Wischer followed through on her idea and established Pinto Well Servicing Company in 1973, she shrewdly decided to capitalize on the feminine touch. She arranged to have all of Pinto's equipment, from backhoes to road graders, painted pink. "It was a new company and I wanted it to be an attention getter, plus I wanted to save advertising costs,'' she says. Her logic was sound: When Pinto took delivery on its new pink Walker-Neer cable tool unit in Wichita Falls, television cameras were on hand. The reaction of the men working on the pink rigs has been, in Wischer's word, ''superb!'' The men have voluntarily taken ''Pinto Pink'' as their slogan and have painted their own small tools to match the rigs. In addition to free advertising, Wischer also accomplished a more subtle objective, ''showing the oil patch country that a woman could do it too and be feminine at the same time.''